CAREER *by Design*

Tips and Tools
for Re-Inventing, Re-Focusing, & Re-Balancing
Your Work-Life

Workbook

2013 Edition

Robin Denise Johnson, Ph.D.

Copyeditor: Margaret A. Ryan
Cover Design: Amy Gonzalez

Published in the United States of America

CAREER BY DESIGN:
TIPS AND TOOLS FOR RE-INVENTING, RE-FOCUSING, & RE-BALANCING YOUR WORK-LIFE

Workbook

2013 Edition

ROBIN DENISE JOHNSON, Ph.D.

Career By Design:
Tips and Tools for
Re-Inventing, Re-Focusing, & Re-Balancing
Your Work-Life

Third Edition

Robin Denise Johnson, Ph.D.

CONTENTS
Career By Design Text

Chapter	Topic	Page
I	INTRODUCTION	9
2	PERSONALITY	19
3	VALUES & NEEDS	37
4	MOTIVATING INTERESTS	63
5	STRENGTHS & SKILLS	83
6	CAREER BY DESIGN MATRIX	105
7	TIPS & TOOLS	121

CONTENTS
Career By Design Worksheets and Tools

Page

Chapter 2: Personality
Worksheet #1: Personality: What's Your Type?   24

Chapter 3: Values And Needs
Worksheet #2: Top Five Values   38
Worksheet #3: Values Clarification Grid   49
Worksheet #4: Voicing Values   51
Worksheet #5a: Work Values   52
Worksheet #5b: Team Values   55

Career by Design Tool #1: Your Mission Statement   56

Chapter 4: Motivating Interests
Worksheet #6: Motivating Interests—20 Things You Love To Do   64
Worksheet #7: Top 10 Motivating Interests   75

Chapter 5: Strengths And Skills
Worksheet #8: Top 10 Skills   88
Worksheet #9: High Interest and Associated Skills   90
Worksheet #10: Skills I Need To Improve   91
Worksheet #11: Skills I Want To Improve   91

Chapter 6: Career By Design Matrix
Worksheet #12: Best Work Skills   108
Worksheet #13: High-Potential Skills   110
Worksheet #14: Supporting Skills   112
Worksheet #15: Low-Level Skills   116

Career By Design Tool #2: Career By Design Matrix   119

Chapter 7: Tips And Tools
Career By Design Tool #3: Mission-Based Decision Matrix   124
Career By Design Tool #4: Career Statements   130
Career By Design Tool #5: Work–Life Balance Ratings   137
Career By Design Tool #6: Time Mastery Scheduling Matrix   145

Career By Design: Tips and Tools for Re-Inventing, Re-Focusing, & Re-Balancing Your Work-Life

CHAPTER 1 - INTRODUCTION

In this program we explore two of life's fundamental questions . . .

Who are you?

and

What do you want?

. . . in order to . . .

- boost your productivity,

- enjoy your work more,

- get promoted and recognized for your contributions,

- develop people who work with you, and

- eliminate energy draining work activities!

Who are you? is a question only you can answer. The activities in this workbook will help you identify and articulate who you are through a series of self-assessment activities. The value of your answers will depend on your honesty and insight as you do each assessment.

Many people do not get what they want because they *don't know* what they want. The question *What do you want?* has different levels of answers.

At the core and deepest level you want to do meaningful work consistent with your personality and purpose. At the next level you want work that enacts your values, or at least enables you to live in ways consistent with your values.

You will only thrive at work if the environment suits your basic needs. When your basic needs are not met, your work is a source of stress.

At the center of your being
you have the answer;
you know who you are and
you know what you want.

—Lao Tzu, <u>Tao Te Ching</u>

At a more conscious level work and long-term career satisfaction are highly correlated with doing daily activities that tap into your motivating interests—not just your superficial interests, but interests that motivate you, that move you physically, emotionally, and psychologically. I would even go so far as to say that you must have those activities that motivate you, if not in your daily work life, then in hobbies, volunteer activities, or community service. In *Career by Design* I will show you how to leverage those motivating interests that may seem impossible to use in your current job.

At a level visible to others you have talents and strengths with which you are born with; things you do naturally. Other people notice them, but these strengths and talents can be so natural to you, like breathing, that you don't notice them. And if you don't know or notice them, you may not develop and use them effectively in your life and career choices.

And then there are the obvious skills. Skills are acquired and developed throughout our lifetimes. Some skills are grounded in our deepest core personality and flow up through our values, needs, motivating interests, and talents. But what I've learned through years of working with people using the *Career by Design* system is that many of us, if not most of us, do what we think we *should* do. We acquire and use skills that we are rewarded for using by salaries, status, and approval from bosses, parents, friends, and spouses. As a result we end up "successful" on the surface but discontent at the core.

At work, your managers will focus on the skills you have that drive the results they desire. And rightly so! That is their job to recognize, use, and reward you for the effective use of skills that contribute to organizational goals. **Your job** is to make sure you are using skills you enjoy using and getting credit for the contributions you make through the intentional use of your skills. Skills, in and of them selves, are not the key driver of career success or career satisfaction. But when skills are like a flower—the visible expression of energy rooted in your unique blend of personality, values, interests, and talents—your work life is truly beautiful.

That is a Career by Design!

Let's cover a few housekeeping items about this program and then we will start you on your journey.

A Note About the *Career By Design* Workbook

The *Career by Design* workbook includes inventories that will enable you to make a realistic assessment of your personality, values, needs, interests, talents, and skills. Most of these assessment instruments can be completed with the written instructions I provide in the workbook. Sometimes I suggest other commercially available assessments because they give you significant and helpful insights.

For assessing personality, needs, and strengths I strongly recommend assessments that must be taken directly from the publishers of those tools—specifically, the Myers–Briggs Type Indicator (MBTI) for personality, the Birkman Method for needs, and StrengthFinders for strengths. If you have already taken these assessments, as many people have, just put the results into the relevant worksheets in this *Career by Design* Workbook. If you have not taken them, I believe the investment in these validated instruments is worth it to gain well-organized insights into yourself. You can do the *Career by Design* process without investing in those assessments, but each of those highly recommended tools will provide you with valuable insights for the rest of your life. They can all be taken online from anywhere in the world. All of them are in English, and most of them are also available in other languages and adjusted for cultural differences.

You can also supplement the assessments inside this workbook with other online tools that are helpful, easily accessed, and widely used. Many people like the DiSC Personality Profiles; FiroB for needs; the Strong Interest Inventory for motivating interests; and SkillScan and the Lominger VOICES 360 feedback system for skills. I am qualified to administer and provide feedback for all of those assessments, as are many other career coaches to whom you may have access through your work or school.

I believe you will get out of the exercises by giving them your full attention. Find a quiet place, print the worksheet for the exercise, and commit pencil to paper.

Your greatest benefit will come from three *Career by Design* tools. These tools help you avoid classic career mistakes.

Career by Design **TOOL #1**: Your personal **Mission Statement** identifies your top values and provides the foundation upon which you can then choose opportunities consistent with those values. This tool, with its associated decision matrix, can help you decide which assignment or job offer to take so that you maximize your career satisfaction. Knowing who you are and what you value is the most important step for making your first and most significant negotiation a successful one: the negotiation for your salary and compensation for your job. Negotiating a $5,000–$10,000 increase in your salary at the beginning of your career can add up to a whopping $1,000,000 over the course of your career.

Career by Design **TOOL #2**: The *Career by Design* **Matrix** will help you determine which items to put on your resume and which skills to talk about in interviews. You can also compare your matrix to the descriptions of jobs you are considering. The matrix may keep you from taking a job just because (1) your parents, friends, or teachers thing you should do that work (but it is not what you really love to do); (2) you have the skills to do the job (but you don't really want to that all day); or (3) because the company is paying you more money than you have ever earned to do that work. (You will discover that the money is not enough to make up for the energy drained by doing boring work.)

Career by Design TOOL #4: The **Career Statement.** There are two variations of the Career Statement: The Career Development Statement and the Career Contribution Statement. The **Career Development Statement** is a good way to prepare for those impromptu conversations when people who could be helpful to your career ask you "What do you do?" It is also a good way to organize your cover letter when you are searching for jobs. The **Career Contribution Statement** focuses your attention and your manager's attention on how you have used your skills and talents to achieve measurable results for your organization. These statements are not resume entries, but rather short, focused statements of intention about who you are, what you have done, and what you want in the future. Your ability to focus on your goals and contributions helps others align with you and support you in your career aspirations.

The other *Career by Design* tools are helpful ones I use frequently in my workshops, so I have included them in this workbook:

Career by Design Tool #3: Mission-Based Decision Matrix

Career by Design Tool #5: Work–Life Balance Ratings Form

Career by Design Tool #6: Time Mastery Scheduling Matrix

This workbook uses assessments to build a strong foundation for your *Career by Design* process. After you have done the assessments in this program, you will be able to target jobs and assignments that are most fulfilling for you, and take goal-directed action in your job search to achieve the career you want. With accurate information about who you are, what you want, and what you do well, you will network more effectively, be more prepared for interviews, negotiate to get your needs met, develop your skills to maximize your choices, and choose jobs, companies, and environments that value your talents and contributions.

A Note to Students

If you are a student considering your first job, you should pay particular attention to the **Personality, Strengths,** and **Motivating Interests** topics in this workbook to help guide you in directions that will be consistent with who you are, your talents, and the work content you are most likely to enjoy. Your career center may also have career interest inventories and can give you additional information about classes that will prepare you for jobs and careers associated with your interests. Do your MBTI personality type assessment through your career center and invest in the book *Do What You Are* for helpful hints about courses to take, skills to develop, internships to consider, and how to approach your job search. While many people may have told you that you can do or be anything you want if you apply yourself, the most effective path to success is to build on strengths and talents you already possess. StrengthFinders helps you do that. For motivating interests you can use the inventories and exercises in this book, but if you have easy access to the Strong Interest Inventory at your school or university, take advantage of that. If you can, get a Birkman Method Career Report. Get an e-version of your report because it will have active links to the Dictionary of Occupational titles with valuable, up-to-date information on career options and outlooks. Because of your phase of life, you may not have accumulated that many skills, but SkillScan will still help you identify the ones you have and think about how to position them as high potential skills for entry-level jobs. One of the most helpful tools in this book will be the **Career Development Statement**, so be sure to do that one.

A Note to People Already Working

While you may already have chosen your job, employer, or business based on your interests, training, education and skills, the ***Career by Design* Matrix** tool in this program will help you refine and enrich your job so that you spend more time doing what you love and what you do well, and less time doing things that drain your energy. This matrix will help you be more strategic in your performance evaluations and negotiate for more resources to support your professional growth. You will know what projects to look for to help you grow and enjoy your work. If you manage other people or work with teams, you will have guidance for managing those relationships more effectively. By using the ***Career by Design* Tool #3: Mission-Based Decision Matrix,** you can select your best career options. And finally, the **Career Contribution Statement** is a fantastic tool for those informal interviews with senior managers, would-be mentors, and potential clients in need of your talents, skills, or services.

A Note to Women and Multicultural Workers

After years of doing research, executive education, and coaching in the diversity and inclusion field, I cannot overestimate the importance of the tools that support strategic career management for so-called demographic minorities. First of all, your long-term career success and enjoyment will be built on the foundation you establish at the beginning of your career. In your early work years you are establishing your credibility and competence. Even if your promotions don't come as quickly as you think they should, a reputation for competence and commitment to your work will circulate in your workplace and serve you in the long run.

Second, choosing work that is grounded in your personal and cultural values and that internally motivates you is very important. Your intrinsic interest in your work will sustain you when you find yourself encountering those inevitable challenges at work, sometimes due to unfair practices, individuals, or companies that have a negative impact on the careers of women and people of color. If you are doing work that is consistent with your values and meaningful for you, then you will also be able to look at yourself in the mirror every day. You will also be able to sit in your rocking chair when you retire and know that you've done your best to make a significant difference in the world. So spend some quality time on the values chapter. So many values and beliefs differ by gender and culture but are invisible. The behaviors grounded in those values and beliefs contribute to work conflict and dissatisfaction. The values information I provide in this workbook can increase your awareness and appreciation of both yours and others' values, thereby reducing much conflict and discontent simply by increasing understanding.

One of the most important decisions you can make

Is to CHOOSE to do what you love to do,

In an environment that allows and values

your contribution as you use your talents and skills.

The Journey Is Yours . . .

The tools in this workbook will provide a compass that you can use in your journey to career effectiveness. The map and the compass are useful, but in the end you have to make the journey—you must take steps to implement what you learn. You'll start taking steps directed toward your goal of an empowered and effective career with this program. But you will continue taking those steps using feedback from your own successes and failures, your body, your colleagues, and your environment to help you stay on the path to career fulfillment.

Your Career by Design

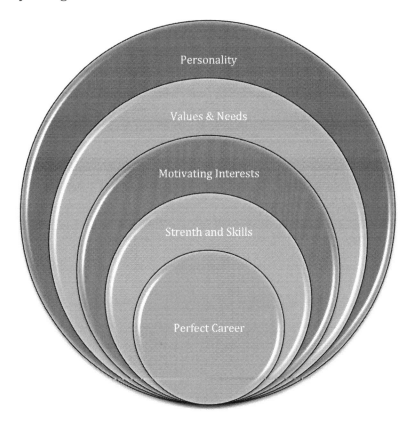

You will be most successful and satisfied in a career that is:

- Grounded in your core personality

- Meaningful because it enacts your individual, social, and cultural values and is done in an environment with relationships that meet your basic needs

- Engages your motivating interests, thereby providing you with energy

- Uses and develops your strengths and rewards you for the contributions you make by using your skills

A *Career by Design* is the result of continuously making high-quality decisions consistent with your personality, values, needs, interests, talents, and skills throughout your life.

Your ideal career will bring all these elements together in a way that is unique for you.

Designing your own career will mean you are more productive, happier with your work and with your coworkers, and growing in a way that gives meaning to your life. You align your head, heart and hands.

CHAPTER 2 - PERSONALITY

Although most career counselors prioritize interests, skills, and values for helping you determine career direction, after years of research and practice I agree with Paul Tieger and Barbara Barron, authors of *Do What You Are*, that the more aspects of your personality you incorporate into your career, the greater your career satisfaction and success. Interests, skills, and values all change with age and life experience. By basing your career on deeper aspects of self (personality and purpose), you need not change careers as your interests, skills, and values change. Your personality is your life blueprint. You are born with it. And it provides a great map that can be used in building the structure of your life, including your career. Behaviors change with situation. The blueprint doesn't.

> *Personality is a set of distinctive individual characteristics, including motives, emotions, values, interests, attitudes, and competencies. Personality is the result of* **personal traits interacting with the environment**.

We map and measure personality through the use of self-report personality inventories, projective tests, and observation from simulations, role plays, and interviews. In using these systems our intention is to be able to identify and articulate individual traits and attributes.

Self-Report Inventories. Self-report inventories require you to answer a series of questions about your behavior. Your responses are then organized in a way that provides insight into some aspect of your personality. Generally these inventories are intended for psychologically healthy people who seek to learn more about themselves and others. There are many personality inventories available. Widely used ones include the Myers–Briggs Type Indicator (MBTI), the Birkman Method, and the DiSC Personality Profiles. I will use the MBTI as the basic personality template here, and I have information about DiSC, Birkman, and a short Personal Traits exercise in the Appendix.

Self-report inventories have the advantage of being readily available, easily interpreted, standardized, and fun to use. Their very subjectivity is appealing to many. They have the disadvantages associated with any self-report instruments: questionable validity/objectivity, a positive self-report bias, and confusing results if the person has ambivalence in his or her personality.

Sensation *tells you that something exists;*
Thinking *tells you what it is;*
Feeling *tells you whether it is agreeable or not;*
and **Intuition** *tells you whence it comes*
and where it is going.

Carl Jung, from <u>Man and His Symbols</u>, p. 61

Jung's Model of Personality: The Foundation for the MBTI

Psychiatrist C. G. Jung developed a typology in his early years in which he theorized that human beings had clear preferences for using two basic cognitive functions—perceiving and judging—and that each function had two styles. Perception could be done in a sensing or intuitive style; judging could be done in a thinking or feeling style. Jung then asserted that those functions were energized by a primarily internally (introverted) or externally (extraverted) directed focus. Jung did this work with individuals in consultations.

Two American women, a mother–daughter team, made two major innovations to Jung's theory. First they developed a forced-choice questionnaire that allowed people to use this theory without going through psychoanalysis. Second, they added another dimension: whether perceiving or judging functions were the cognitive functions a person showed the outer world. Their instrument is named after them: the Myers–Briggs Type Indicator (MBTI). Although there is a lot of research using the MBTI, much of its power comes from its *face validity*, which means that people believe that the instrument gives them accurate information about their personality.

Two other behavioral psychologists liked the MBTI but wanted to add more behavioral objective research to its validity. These psychologists, Keirsey and Bates, found that they could not find statistically significant results regarding behaviors for all 16 types that come from the MBTI, but they could support four combinations of styles, which they then termed *temperaments*. Thus this personality tool has these major contributory sources: C. G. Jung, Isabel Briggs–Myers and her mother Katherine Briggs, plus David Keirsey and Marilyn Bates.

Jungian types are based on four preferences that answer the following questions:

1.   From where does your primary source of energy come? (Extraversion–Introversion)
2.   How do you prefer to take in information? (Sensation–Intuition)
3.   How do you prefer to make judgments/decisions? (Thinking–Feeling)
4.   How do you prefer to organize your life? (Judging–Perceiving)

Sensing, Intuiting, Thinking and Feeling are the four cognitive function styles in Jungian typology. Unlike many other psychological personality assessment tools, the Jungian Myers–Briggs and Keirsey–Bates indicators do not search for psychological problems. It is arguably the most widely used personality system in the world today, in part because it elicits valuable data-gathering and decision-making preferences for normal, healthy people.

The 8-Word Language. When you encounter people who have used the MBTI, they will frequently use various letters to refer to personality styles. You'll hear "I'm an INTJ," or "She's an ESFP," etc. What are they talking about?!?

S–N:
THE PERCEIVING FUNCTIONS:
SENSING AND INTUITING

The irrational functions. How you prefer to take in information, find out about things, and the data you are most likely to notice. What you pay attention to . . .

When you take in facts or details, you are using your Sensation faculties, denoted by the letter *S*. When you pay attention to patterns or overviews, you are using your iNtuition, denoted by the letter *N* (*N* is used to avoid confusion with *I*ntroversion). If you prefer facts and details, MBTI says you have a Sensing preference—you prefer information taken in primarily by way of your five senses. If you pay more attention to patterns, MBTI would say you have a preference for iNtuition—for gaining information perceived primarily through the "sixth" sense.

T–F:
THE JUDGING FUNCTIONS:
THINKING AND FEELING

The rational functions. How you prefer to make decisions. The process you use to make decisions . . .

If you prefer to make decisions from an objective distance, impersonally considering causes and events, in MBTI you have a preference for Thinking, denoted by the letter *T*. If you prefer to make decisions up close and personal—to make values-based decisions considering the impact of those decisions on yourself and others—in MBTI you have a Feeling preference, denoted by the letter *F*. In the United States there is a gender difference on T and F preferences, with approximately 2/3 of women having an F preference and 2/3 of men having a T preference. Among managers in business, however, a very high percentage of both women and men have a T preference. Based on data collected so far, men within any given national culture report a T preference with 10–25% greater frequency than women do in the same culture, but very few cultures have as great a difference in this preference as we see in the United States. One way to test your personality preference on this dimension is to think about what you do/address first. T's are known to address problems or tasks first and people second; F's are inclined to deal with people issues first.

E–I:
THE DIRECTION OF ENERGY FLOW:
EXTRAVERSION–INTROVERSION

The attitude that colors the functions. How you are energized and where you prefer to focus your attention . . .

If you gain energy from the outer world of activity or words, you would have an MBTI personality preference for Extraversion, denoted by the letter *E*. If you gain energy from your inner world of contemplation, or thoughts, your preference would be called Introversion, denoted by the letter *I*. *Extra-* is a prefix meaning "without" and *intro-* is a prefix meaning "within." Many extraverts say they find social interactions with lots of people energizing. Introverts frequently report feeling drained in such situations. It is important to remember that introversion is not shyness or timidity. Most introverts are selectively sociable. Introverts tend to prefer one-on-one interactions and need time to trust you before opening up.

While we find cultural differences in the preferences for introversion and extraversion, globally this scale is about 50/50. However, the dominant preference is the United States is for extraversion. So extraverts, if you are interacting with an introvert, ask your question and wait few 7 seconds before jumping in again. This gives introverts time to think and give their best answer. Introverts, remember that the conversation in your heads needs to be spoken aloud, maybe repeated, for extraverts to know what you are thinking.

J–P:
THE FUNCTION USED IN THE OUTER WORLD:
JUDGING OR PERCEIVING

The type of function you show the outer world. Lifestyle you adopt . . .

If you organize your life in a structured way, making decisions and knowing where you stand, then you likely have a Judgment preference, denoted by the letter *J*. If you like to keep things flexible, discovering life as you go along, then your preference may be for Perception, denoted by the letter *P*. These terms refer to which of your cognitive preferences you use in the outer world. Do you show your perceiving data-gathering function (S or N) by wanting more information and considering lots of options (P at the end)? Or do you show your decision-making function (T or F) by coming to closure and organizing people, events, and ideas fairly quickly (J at the end)?

J's are known to believe deadlines and occasionally get upset with P's for their different attitude toward deadlines. Both actually can work to deadlines, but for P's the path may include some diversions, and it's the REAL rather than the convenient deadline that matters to P's. If P's produce to real deadlines, leave them alone. If not, discuss and agree on some form of organization, but it may not necessarily be the J's form. If a P misses a deadline, give him or her firm feedback and let the person live with the consequences.

WORKSHEET #1: Personality: What's Your Type?

Circle the four letters you believe to be your personality type: E or I, S or N, T or F, J or P. You are capable of using all the styles, but this exercise is about which of the two you prefer if you tap into your inner knowing and do what comes most naturally for you. If you have already taken the MBTI, just circle the four descriptions associated with your four-letter type code based on your MBTI results.

E   Extraversion

People who prefer Extraversion tend to focus on the outer world of people and things.

I   Introversion

People who prefer Introversion tend to focus on the inner world of ideas and impressions.

S   Sensing

People who prefer Sensing tend to focus on the present and on concrete information gained from their senses.

N   iNtuition

People who prefer Intuition tend to focus on the future, with a view toward patterns and possibilities.

T   Thinking

People who prefer Thinking tend to base their decisions on logic and on objective analysis of cause and effect.

F   Feeling

People who prefer Feeling tend to base their decisions primarily on values and on subjective evaluation of person-centered concerns.

J   Judging

People who prefer Judging tend to like a planned and organized approach to life and prefer to have things settled.

P   Perceiving

People who prefer Perceiving tend to like a flexible and spontaneous approach to life and prefer to keep their options open.

Write your four-letter type code here: ____   ____   ____   ____

E or I   S or N   T or F   J or P

Personality Type Work and Communication Styles

The chart below provides some information about how you might prefer to work, given your personality type. In the chart below your possible work style is in normal font, and your *communication preferences* are *italicized*.

Extraversion—E	Introversion—I
Like variety, action Impatient with long, slow jobs Intrinsic value of work important Act quickly Phone calls welcome diversion Develop ideas through discussion Like having people around *Respond quickly, talk over others* *High energy, high animation* *Seek and use opportunities to speak in groups* *Prefer face-to-face over written communication* *In meetings, like to talk things over out loud before reaching a conclusion*	Like quiet for concentration Prefer to work on one project for a long time without interruptions Are interested in the ideas behind/under their work Think before they act; sometimes don't act Like working alone *Like to think before responding* *Focus on internal ideas and thoughts* *Need space to share ideas out loud* *Seek and prefer to talk one-on-one* *Prefer written over face-to-face communications* *In meetings may verbalize well thought-out conclusions or summarize key ideas*
Sensing—S	Intuition—N
Use (past) experience to solve problems Enjoy applying what they learn; practical learners and problem solvers Seldom make (and always dislike) factual errors Prefer details first, then big picture Fine-tune; innovate from what is Prefer step-by-step procedures Temperamentally inclined to conserve rather than change *Like facts, details, evidence, data first.* *Want practical, realistic applications shown* *Rely on direct-experience anecdotes* *Use step-by-step approach in presentations* *Clear, straightforward, feasible suggestions* *Refer to specific examples* *Inclined to follow meeting agenda*	Enjoy new, complex problems, new skills Enjoy learning new skills more than using the new skill—learning is an end itself May follow inspirations, hunches Vision more important than fact Multiple truths/perspectives valued Like overview first, then details Prefer change (sometimes radical) to continuation of what is; temperamentally inclined to act as change agents Usually proceed in bursts of energy *Like global schemes, with broad issues addressed and presented first* *Want possible future challenges discussed ("what if" analysis) to provoke discussion* *Like novel, unusual ideas and approaches* *Use agenda only as starting point for discussion in meetings*

Thinking—T	Feeling—F
Use logical analysis to reach conclusions	Use values for decision-making
Can work/play without harmony—pick who's best for the team; does not need to like them	Work best in harmonious environment with people they like
Impersonal decisions, principled	Enjoy pleasing people
Task first, reward when done	May avoid telling people unpleasant things
Job well done is its own reward	Look at the underlying values in situations
	Feel rewarded when human needs met
Concise, brief, bottom-line style	*Prefer sociable, friendly interactions (use courtesy rituals, chat, connect)*
Bulleted lists of pros and cons listed	*Want to know why an option is valuable and how it affects people who have a stake*
Critique appreciated, objectivity preferred	*Convinced by personal information, delivered enthusiastically*
Present goals and objectives first	*Present points of agreement first*
Emotions or feelings are data to weigh	*Consider logic and objectivity as data to link to values*
Task focus in meetings	*Seek to involve people in meetings*
	Appreciate people in the meeting and give credit to those who have helped

Judging—J	Perceiving—P
Plan, then follow that plan	Multi-taskers
Like to complete tasks	Improvisers, like flexibility in work, adapt
Focused	Like to leave things open for last-minute changes
Tend to be satisfied once they've reached a decision on a thing, person, situation, task	Tend to be curious and welcome new info about people, things, situations
Seek and use structure, goals, schedules, plans	Feel restricted without change
Use lists to prompt action on specific tasks	
Want to discuss schedules and timetables and have tight deadlines	*Willing to discuss timelines and schedules but are uncomfortable if they are too tight, too rigid*
Dislike surprises, give advance warning of changes	*Enjoy surprises and like adapting to last-minute changes and incorporating new information*
Expect others to follow through; account-ability is important	*Expect others to adapt to situational requirements*
State positions and decisions clearly	*Communicate options and opportunities*
Communicate results and achievements	*Present views as tentative and modifiable*
Talk of purpose and direction	*Talk of autonomy and flexibility*
Communicate alternatives	*Process orientation in meetings*
Stay focused on task in meetings	

Personality Type and Careers

The following list is a sampling of careers and jobs that either attract people with that personality type or use the preferences of that type. Any personality type can do any job. This is not a list of the "only jobs you can do," but simply a guide to which career utilizes the natural talents of each type. If your chosen career is not listed under a particular type . .

- It does not mean that you cannot do that kind of work.
- It does not mean that you would not enjoy that kind of work.
- It does not mean that you cannot make a contribution doing that kind of work.

The careers listed are just to help you consider how your ways of using energy, gathering data, and making decisions might influence your productivity, learning, and satisfaction with a career choice. What is more important, is to discuss your career goals and reasoning with your career counselor, HR professional, manager, or coach. At the end of each career list you will see a reason why people with that personality type are attracted to the careers listed for that personality.

Observant (S)							
Judging				*Probing*			
Guardians				Artisans			
Thinking		Feeling		Thinking		Feeling	
ESTJ	**ISTJ**	**ESFJ**	**ISFJ**	**ESTP**	**ISTP**	**ESFP**	**ISFP**
Manager	Inspector	Provider	Protector	Promoter	Crafter	Composer	Performer

Introspective (N)							
Thinking				*Feeling*			
Rationals				Idealists			
Judging		Probing		Judging		Probing	
ENTJ	**INTJ**	**ENTP**	**INTP**	**ENFJ**	**INFJ**	**ENFP**	**INFP**
General	Mastermind	Inventor	Architect	Mentor	Counselor	Champion	Healer

ESTJ. Military, business administrators, managers, police, detective work, judges, financial officers, teachers, sales representatives, government workers, insurance agents, underwriters, nursing administrators, trade and technical teachers.

*ESTJs have a lot of flexibility in the types of careers that they choose. They are good at a lot of different things, because they put forth a tremendous amount of effort toward doing things the right way. They will be happiest in leadership positions, however, because they have a natural drive to be in charge. They make their most substantial contributions by creating order and structure from apparent chaos. Natural leaders, they work best when they are in charge and enforcing the rules.

ISTJ. Business executives, administrators and managers, accountants, police, detectives, judges, lawyers, medical doctors, dentists, computer programmers, systems analysts, computer specialists, auditors, electricians, math teachers, mechanical engineers, steelworkers, technicians, militia members.

*ISTJs are the *duty fulfillers*. Similar to the ESTJs, they have a knack for detail and memorization, but may prefer to work more behind the scenes instead of up front as a leader. ISTJs have one character trait that is a definite advantage in terms of career success: perseverance. ISTJs can do almost anything that they have decided to do. However, there are areas in which they will function more happily and naturally. ISTJs can make great contributions using their excellent organizational skills and their powers of concentration to create order and structure.

ESFJ. Home economics, nursing, teaching, administrators, child care, family practice physician, clergy, office managers, counselors, social workers, bookkeeping, accounting, secretaries, organization leaders, dental assistants, homemakers, radiological technologists, receptionists, religious educators, speech pathologists.

*ESFJs are the *caregivers*. They have two primary traits that will help define their best career contributions: (1) they are extremely organized and enjoy creating order, and (2) much of their self-satisfaction is gotten through giving and helping others. Accordingly, they tend to contribute in tangible ways by creating or maintaining order and structure that serve others. They do best in jobs where they can apply their natural warmth at building relationships with other people.

ISFJ. Interior decorators, designers, nurses, administrators, managers, secretaries, child care, early childhood development, social work, counselors, paralegals, clergy, office managers, shopkeepers, bookkeepers, homemakers, gardeners, clerical supervisors, curators, family practice physicians, health service workers, librarians, medical technologists, typists.

*ISFJs are the *nurturers*. They have two basic traits that help their careers: (1) they are extremely interested and in-tune with how other people are feeling, and (2) they enjoy creating structure and order, and are extremely good at it. Ideally, ISFJs will use their exceptional people-observation skills to determine what people want or need, and then use their excellent organizational abilities to create a structured plan or environment for achieving what people want. Their excellent sense of space and function combined with their awareness of aesthetic quality also gives them quite special abilities in the more practical artistic endeavors. Tradition-oriented and down-to-earth, they do best in jobs where they can help people achieve their goals, or where structure is needed.

ESTP. Sales representatives, marketers, police, detectives, paramedics, medical technicians, computer technicians, computer technical support, entrepreneurs, comedians, agents, race car drivers, firefighters, military, auditors, carpenters, craft workers, farmers, laborers, service workers, transportation operatives.

*ESTPs are the *doers*. They have some advantageous traits that are unique to their personality type. Their observation skills make them extremely good at correctly analyzing and assessing other peoples' motives or perspectives. Their people skills allow them to use this knowledge to their advantage while interacting with people. For this reason, ESTPs are excellent salespeople. They also have a special ability to react quickly and effectively to an immediate need, such as in an emergency or crisis situation. This is a valuable skill in many different professions, perhaps most notably in action-oriented professions, such as police work. ESTPs enjoy new experiences and dealing with people, and dislike being confined in structured or regimented environments. They also want to see an immediate result for their actions, and don't like dealing with a lot of high-level theory where that won't be the case. For these reasons, their contributions are most notable when they have regular interactions with people, clear action-oriented goals, and limited analysis–paralysis with routine, detailed tasks. They have a gift for reacting to and solving immediate problems and persuading other people.

ISTP. Police, detectives, forensic pathologists, computer programmers, system analysts, computer specialists, engineers, carpenters, mechanics, pilots, drivers, athletes, entrepreneurs, firefighters, paramedics, construction workers, dental hygienists, electrical engineers, farmers, military, probation officers, steelworkers, and transportation operatives.

*ISTPs are the *mechanics*. ISTPs have the ability to be good at many different kinds of tasks. Their introverted and thinking preferences give them the ability to concentrate and work through problems. However, ISTPs work best when they have a great deal of autonomy, working for themselves, or working in very flexible environments. Their natural interests lie toward applying their excellent reasoning skills against known facts and data to discover underlying structure or solutions to practical questions. With the ability to stay calm under pressure, they excel in any job that requires immediate action.

ESFP. Actors, painters, comedians, entertainers, sales representatives, teachers, counselors, social workers, child care, fashion designers, interior decorators, consultants, photographers, musicians, human resources managers, clerical supervisors, coaches, factory supervisors, food service workers, receptionists, recreation workers, religious educators, respiratory therapists.

* ESFPs are the *performers*. ESFPs are good at many things, but will not be happy unless they have a lot of contact with people, and many new experiences. They contribute most through using their great people skills and practical perspective in environments that offer sufficient new challenges that they will not become bored. Optimistic and fun-loving, their enthusiasm is great for motivating others.

ISFP. Artists, musicians, composers, designers, child care workers, social workers, counselors, teachers, veterinarians, forest rangers, naturalists, bookkeepers, carpenters, clerical supervisors, secretaries, dental and medical staffers, waiters and waitresses, chefs, nurses, mechanics, physical therapists, X-ray technicians.

*ISFPs are the *artists*. They are individuals who need to believe that their work is more than a job. The middle of the road is not likely to be a place where they will be fulfilled and happy. They need to do work that is consistent with their strong core of inner values. Since they prefer to live in the current moment and to take the time to savor it, they do not do well with some of the more fast-paced corporate environments. They need a great deal of space that gives free reign to their natural abilities, where they may find a wonderful artist within themselves. Many of the world's major artists have been ISFP. And since ISFPs are so acutely aware of people's feelings and reactions, and are driven by their inner values to help people, ISFPs may find themselves making a difference by coaching, counseling, mentoring, and teaching. They tend to do well in the arts, as well as in helping professions that work with people.

ENFJ. Teachers, consultants, psychiatrists, social workers, counselors, clergy, sales representatives, human resources, managers, events coordinators, politicians, diplomats, writers, actors, designers, homemakers, musicians, religious workers.

*ENFJs are the *givers*. They are genuinely and warmly interested in people, value harmony and structure, dislike impersonal logic and analysis, are creative and imaginative, enjoy variety and new challenges, get personal satisfaction from helping others, are extremely sensitive to criticism and discord, and need approval from others to feel good about themselves. The range of these characteristics leave the ENFJs a lot of leeway in choosing a profession and making a contribution. As long as they're in a supportive environment in which they can work with people and are presented with sufficiently diverse challenges to stimulate their creativity, they do very well. They have a gift of encouraging others to actualize themselves, and they provide excellent leadership.

INFJ. Counselors, clergy, missionaries, teachers, medical doctors, dentists, chiropractors, psychologists, psychiatrists, writers, musicians, artists, psychics, photographers, child care workers, education consultants, librarians, marketers, scientists, social workers.

*INFJs are the *protectors*. INFJs need meaning in their work. They need to feel as if everything they do in their lives is in sync with their strong value systems, with what they believe to be right. Accordingly, INFJs should choose work where they contribute in a way that is consistent with their deeply held principles and that supports them in their life quest to be doing something meaningful. INFJs must know and live according to their values. Since INFJs have such strong value systems and persistent intuitive visions that lend them a sense of "knowing," they do best in positions in which they are leaders, rather than followers. Although they can happily follow individuals who are leading in a direction that INFJs fully support, they will be very unhappy following in any other situation. Blessed with an idealistic vision, they do best when they seek to make that vision a reality.

ENFP. Actors, journalists, writers, musicians, painters, consultants, psychologists, psychiatrists, entrepreneurs, teachers, counselors, politicans, diplomats, television reporters, marketers, scientists, sales representatives, artists, clergy, public relations, social scientists, social workers.

*ENFPs are the *inspirers*. They are project-oriented, dislike performing routine tasks, and need approval and appreciation from others. They have well-developed communication skills, are natural leaders, but do not like to control people and resist being controlled by others. They can work logically and rationally, using their intuition to understand the goal and work backward toward it. ENFPs tend to be good a quite a lot of different things and can generally achieve a good degree of success at anything that has interested them. However, ENFPs get bored rather easily and may not naturally follow things through to completion. Accordingly, they generally avoid jobs that require performing a lot of detailed, routine-oriented tasks. They will do best in professions that allow them to creatively generate new ideas and deal closely with people. They are rarely happy in positions that are confining and regimented. Very creative and fun-loving, they excel at careers that allow them to express their ideas and spontaneity.

INFP. Writers, artists, counselors, social workers, English teachers, fine arts teachers, child care workers, clergy, missionaries, psychologists, psychiatrists, scientists, political activists, editors, education consultants, journalists, religious educators, social scientists.

*INFPs are the *idealists*. They are sensitive individuals who also need to find meaning in their work. INFPs need to feel that everything they do in their lives is in accordance with their strongly felt value systems and is moving themselves and others in a positive, growth-oriented direction. They tend to be flexible and laid back, unless one of their core values is violated. They are driven to do something purposeful with their lives. INFPs are happiest when they can live their daily lives in accordance with their values, and work toward the greater good of humanity. It is worth mentioning that many of the truly great writers in the world have been INFPs. Driven by a strong sense of personal values, they are also highly creative and can offer support from behind the scenes.

ENTJ. Business executives, CEOs, organization founders, business administrators, managers, entrepreneurs, judges, lawyers, computer consultants, university professors, politicians, credit investigators, labor relations worker, marketing department manager, mortgage banker, systems analysts, scientists.

*ENTJs are the *executives*. They are especially well suited to be leaders and organization builders because they have the ability to clearly identify problems and innovative solutions for the short- and long-term well-being of an organization. Having a strong desire to lead, they're not likely to be happy as followers. ENTJs like to be in charge, and they *need* to be in charge to take advantage of their special capabilities. They are born to lead and can steer the organization toward their vision, using their excellent organizational skills and understanding of what needs to get done.

INTJ. Scientists, engineers, professors, teachers, medical doctors, dentists, corporate strategists, organization founders, business administrators, managers, military, lawyers, judges, computer programmers, system analysts, computer specialists, psychologists, photographers, research department managers, researchers, university instructors, chess players.

*INTJs are the *scientists*. More so than any other personality type, INTJs are brilliant when it comes to grasping complex theories and applying them to problems to come up with long-term strategies. This type of "strategizing" is the central focus and drive of the INTJ. Accordingly, INTJs are happiest and most effective in environments that allow this type of processing, and where they are given a lot of autonomy over their daily lives. They have a particular inclination for grasping difficult, complex concepts and for building strategies.

ENTP. Entrepreneurs, lawyers, psychologists, photographers, consultants, sales representatives, actors, engineers, scientists, inventors, marketers, computer programmers, comedians, computer analysts, credit investigators, journalists, psychiatrists, public relations, designers, writers, artists, musicians, politicians.
*ENTPs are the *visionaries*. They are fortunate in that they have a wide range of capabilities and are generally good at anything that has captured their interest. ENTPs are likely to be successful in many different careers. Since they have a lot of options open to them, ENTPs will do well to choose professions that allow them a lot of personal freedom where they can use their creativity to generate new ideas and solve problems. They will not be completely happy in positions that are regimented or confining. Very freedom-oriented, they need a career that allows them to act independently and to freely express their creativity and insight.

INTP. Physicists, chemists, biologists, photographers, strategic planners, mathematicians, university professors, computer programmers, computer animators, technical writers, engineers, lawyers, forensic researchers, writers, artists, psychologists, social scientists, systems analysts, researchers, surveyors.
*INTPs are the *thinkers*. They have a gift for generating and analyzing theories and possibilities to prove or disprove them. They have a great deal of insight and are creative thinkers, which allows them to quickly grasp complex abstract thoughts. They also have exceptional logical and rational reasoning skills, which allow them to thoroughly analyze theories to discover he truth about them. They have their own very high standards, and they value knowledge and competence above all else. INTPs will be happiest with a great deal of autonomy, in which they can work primarily alone on developing and analyzing complex theories and abstractions, with the goal of their work being the discovery of a truth, rather than the discovery of a practical application. Highly analytical, they can discover connections between two seemingly unrelated phenomena, and work best when allowed to use their imagination and critical thinking.

Remember! If your chosen career is not listed under that type, it does NOT mean that you cannot do that kind of work, it does NOT mean that you would not enjoy that kind of work, and it does NOT mean that you cannot make a contribution doing that kind of work. Pay more attention to *why* the career might appeal to those personalities, than to the jobs themselves. For a far more in-depth discussion of why a career might work for your personality type, I highly recommend the book *Do What You Are* by Paul Tieger and Barbara Baron.

The MBTI has been used for research in more than 30 countries and has over 21 translations and cultural adaptations. Researchers find all the types in all these countries around the world. And the research shows that people in similar occupations, no matter where they live in the world, will often have personality types similar to people in other countries in the same occupation.

Get your MBTI Step II Report.
Contact someone certified to administer it - your HR department,
your Campus Career Center, CPP directly, or me.

Your Step II report provides information with
practical applications of the MBTI, especially for
communication,
decision-making,
change management, and
conflict management.

If you do not have the resources or access to a
certified MBTI administrator, there are also a
number of free adaptations of the MBTI available
online.

MBTI Subscales

One of the most common critiques of the 16-type MBTI is that people feel there are not enough factors to capture their unique personality. The MBTI Step II Report addresses that concern with the addition of subscales. The Step II Report breaks down the 4 dichotomous MBTI scales into 20 subscales. As a result there are not just 16 different personality types, but over a million permutations of preferences. These subscales begin to capture our multifaceted personalities. They are . . .

EXTRAVERSION (E)	INTROVERSION (I)	SENSING (S)	INTUITION (N)
initiating	receiving	concrete	abstract
expressive	contained	realistic	imaginative
gregarious	intimate	practical	conceptual
active	reflective	experiential	theoretical
enthusiastic	quiet	traditional	original

THINKING (T)	FEELING (F)	JUDGING (J)	PERCEIVING (P)
logical	empathetic	systematic	casual
reasonable	compassionate	planful	open-ended
questioning	accommodating	early-starting	pressure-prompted
critical	accepting	scheduled	spontaneous
tough	tender	methodical	emergent

So, although I am introverted (by MBTI and self-validation), I am outside of that description on one facet: I am also expressive. In the MBTI Step II report, then, my personality type says that I am an *expressive introvert*. This refinement of personality type is particularly helpful as you start to target specific jobs. Understanding that I am an expressive introvert, for instance, explains why I enjoy doing presentations and teaching, but also why I need time alone to recharge after I have just done a large program. By personality, I have a preference for both introversion and expression. In my case, aside from expressiveness, which is on the extraverted side of the E–I personality continuum, I tend to see my personality more in line with introverted subscales—receiving, intimate, reflective, and quiet.

CHAPTER 3 - VALUES & NEEDS

Values are principles and standards that are important to you.

You may have individual values, and you may share values with others in your family, organization, or culture. Values are deeply held and strongly felt—you have an emotional and psychological investment in them.

In the values assessments you will do here, you'll be determining **your** values—not what you should or should not think–feel–do based on what your parents, the media, your teachers, or your religion taught you, or what other people around you assume you value. You will be identifying and prioritizing what is important to **you**. You may have had some values when you were younger that have changed as you matured, after you have had different life experiences and different responsibilities. Values, and value priorities, will change during your lifetime.

The process of identifying and working with your values involves several steps, for which I have provided worksheets to guide you through the process.

WORKSHEET #2: Top Five Values. You will select your top five values from the **Values Inventory** and define–refine each value for yourself.

WORKSHEET #3: Values Clarification Grid. In this exercise you will differentiate espoused (talked about) values from enacted (lived) values. You will also share your top five values with at least one other person.

WORKSHEET #4: Voicing Values. In this exercise you will define your top five values and tell at least one other person, out loud, what those values are. In addition, share your intent to live your life according to your top five values.

WORKSHEETS #5a and #5b: Work & Team Values. In addition to your top five life values, there are values that make a positive difference in your work experience. On these worksheets you will identify those values. There are two variations for work values - a general work values sheet using the same long list of values from the values inventory, plus a team values worksheet listing values that make a significant difference when people are working together.

***CAREER BY DESIGN* TOOL #1: Mission Statement**. Crafting and memorizing your personal mission statement helps you remember your top five values and make decisions consistent with those values. In Chapter 7 I provide a tool and tips for using this mission statement when you're trying to decide which project to do, or job to take.

The last section of this chapter describes the power of needs and the environments that are most likely to support you in doing your best work. Needs are part of the psychological contract between you and your workplace. I suggest using the Birkman Method assessment to identify and articulate your needs.

WORKSHEET #2: Top Five Values

Step 1. Select your top five values from the VALUES INVENTORY that starts on the next page. The list is alphabetical. If you have more than five values, be rigorous and choose only five for this worksheet. In the Work Values Worksheet #5 that comes later, you will be able to select more values. The hard part of this exercise is selecting *only five values*. These five will be your guide. You may prioritize them if you wish, but that is not required at this point.

VALUE	WHAT THIS VALUE MEANS TO ME
1	
2	
3	
4	
5	

VALUES INVENTORY

The VALUES INVENTORY includes cultural, individual, work, and personal values. All of the values are positive. As you select your values, you will simultaneously learn about others' values. You need not agree with others' values, but it is helpful to know what the values alternatives are so that you can choose your own values (and respect others' when you need to do so). If you believe one of your top 5 values is missing from the VALUES INVENTORY, there is space to write that value in at the end. You may also include that value on **WORKSHEET #2: Top Five Values**.

	Acceptance – be accepted as you are for who you are
	Access – live and work where the playing field is even and provides access to what is needed for a quality life
	Accuracy – use data in ways that get consistent, verifiable results
	Achievement - succeeding in doing something based on effort expended; an internal standard of excellence in all that you do
	Advancement – have challenges and opportunities where you can take risks, demonstrate ability, and win/compete to gain higher status or better position
	Adventure - undertaking activities that provide excitement and extraordinary events; seeking and being willing to participate in things that involve risk and uncertainty
	Aging well - changing with time, maturing when growing older in life
	Altruism – selfless concern for the well-being of others
	Artistic expression – sharing processes and products of human skill, imagination, and invention with the world
	Authority – the legitimate right to make decisions based on position power
	Autonomy - have personal control over your tasks and time
	Beauty/aesthetics – make life more beautiful or have time to appreciate beautiful things
	Being - thinking, contemplating are valuable; self-definition based on "who I am" regardless of external accomplishment
	Birthright - family background and heritage are essential self-defining qualities.
	Challenge – invent or revitalize thoughts, ideas, processes, or approaches that prove your abilities and help you grow
	Change - seen as positive, healthy, natural; it represents growth; "new and improved" concept
	Charity - voluntary sharing; giving money, materials, support, kindness, and resources to people in need
	Cleanliness – the state of being free from dirt, and the process of achieving and maintaining that state
	Comfort - being, feeling relaxed; free from pain and anxiety
	Commitment – keeping your word and agreements to self and others

Communication – being effective in letting others know what you think and feel
Community – commitment to the shared responsibilities and connections in the area you live, of the groups to which you belong
Compassion – a motivational state associated with the propensity to actively relieve the suffering of others
Competence – possessing and using skills, knowledge, qualities, and capacity to do something well
Competition –competition is healthy and brings out the best in people
Conservation – to protect all life forms—animals, fungi, plants, people—and their habitats
Conservatism – disposed to preserve existing conditions, institutions, or to restore traditional ones and limit change so that it is moderate and purposeful
Context/place - physical, geographic, historical, cultural, and temporal contexts are meaningful and important to life
Contribution – have your work, life, presence on the planet make a difference
Cosmopolitan – global citizenship; awareness of and connection to how events affect entire world population
Courage – ability and willingness to take action even when it is risky or even life-threatening
Creativity – allow your imagination to find new, unique ways to express ideas, thoughts
Curiosity – explore new areas of knowledge and awareness; seek new understanding
Democracy – the right of every one to contribute to the governance of nations, organizations, and communities
Detail – thorough and attentive to particular and specific parts or processes
Dignity – maintaining poise and a sense of self, no matter what
Direct communication - honest, open, get to the point
Discipline – calm, controlled, conscious behavior; systematic approach to behavior, activity, subject, or lifestyle
Discovery - finding out about things for the first time; finding something new or unexpected after searching

	Diversity – seeking and valuing contact with those who are different from you; believe variety enhances your life experience
	Doing/activity orientation — hard work pays off; prefer action over contemplation of ideas; self-worth based on what you do or accomplish with your life
	Duty – carry out your responsibilities and commitments.
	Empathy – an emotional sensitivity to the needs and wants of others
	Empiricism – belief in knowledge acquired through sensory, objective, verified, quantified, scientific methods and experimentation
	Equality/egalitarianism – belief that all people are equal and should have equal access to things they need in life; treat everyone the same; believe people are (should be) free to change their roles
	Excellence – an internal high standard for doing/achieving things in life
	Expertise – to value and be valued for your knowledge, wisdom, experience, scholarly or intellectual abilities
	Expressiveness – share your unique ideas, feelings, and talents with others
	Extraversion – deriving energy from the outer world of people, objects, and events that involves initiating, expression, gregariousness, activity, and enthusiasm
	Extrinsic religiosity - religion helps us obtain desired goals, personal comfort, and social status consistent with God's wish for us
	Fairness - demonstrating impartial, unbiased, and equitable treatment to others; giving to each according to what they need, earned, or deserve
	Faith – a strong belief in a higher intelligence that guides, sustains your life
	Family – having a strong commitment to people with whom you share bonds of blood and marriage
	Fate - external forces (e.g., God, fate, genetics) control humankind, and many things are beyond our control because they are hereditary or in God's hands, etc.
	Financial freedom - having enough financial resources to support your lifestyle; no debt; working because you want to, not because you have to
	Formality - ritual and tradition are valued; formality is a sign of respect and importance
	Freedom/autonomy – have open-ended responsibilities with ability to choose and define your life, love, and work

	Friendship – personal relationships grounded in mutual concern for each other
	Fundamentalism – only one set of religious teachings (the Bible, the Torah, the Koran, etc.) clearly contains the fundamental, basic, intrinsic, essential, inerrant truth about humanity and God; this essential truth is fundamentally opposed by forces of evil that must be vigorously fought; this truth must be followed today using basic, unchangeable practices from the past; and following these fundamental teachings creates a special relationship with God/Jesus/Allah/Yahweh
	Future - planning ahead, goal setting, working today for a better future
	Generosity – willingness to share time, treasures, talents with others without viewing it as a transactional exchange for something in return
	Group/collectivism - strong identification with others; think interdependency with others is normal and desirable
	Growth –in personal terms, to have opportunities to improve yourself and self-actualize; professionally, to seek to enhance your skills and experience
	Harmony – seeking, contributing to, and maintaining conflict-free relations between people; "all for one, and one for all"
	Healing – helping others become healthy or maintain their health
	Help others – Give support, advice, information, or assistance to people, animals, groups, or organizations
	Hierarchy – View rank, status, and title as important; we should treat people differently according to their place in society; specific rights, obligations, and personality characteristics are expected based on age, sex, and position within society
	Honesty – telling the truth about your life and experience
	Human interaction - personal relationships with people are important
	Humility - being modest and respectful
	Idealism – cherishing or pursuit of high and noble principles and goals
	Immanence spirituality – belief that everything is God/part of the universe; transcendence of interpersonal and intrapersonal boundaries is good
	Independence – making decisions and carrying them out without regard or need for others' assistance or approval
	Indirect communication - subtle, delicate, inferred communication that respects people's intelligence and ability to decipher meaning while saving face

Individuality – free to be yourself and express yourself in your own unique manner; see privacy as necessary and desirable; see each person as unique/special
Influence – have an impact on the opinions, decisions, lives of others
Informality - casual and spontaneous behavior is appreciated
Initiative – taking action on your own without waiting for approval or permission
Innovation – creating new and different objects, ideas, and experiences
Integrity – consistency in word, thought, and deed in your interactions
Intellectual challenge – explore ideas, problems, puzzles, or decisions that test your mental abilities, creativity, knowledge, assumptions, or world views; competitive tests of mental prowess against other intellectuals
Introversion – deriving energy from your inner world of thoughts, feelings, and ideas; being receptive, contained, intimate, reflective, or quiet
Intrinsic religiosity – believe people should *live* their religion; orthodoxy is valued
Joy – happiness, contentment, pleasure (especially of an elevated or spiritual kind)
Justice - fairness or reasonableness in the way people are treated, the decisions made, and the result/impact
Kindness – good and charitable behavior, pleasant disposition, concern for others
Knowledge/expertise - contribute to new findings in technology, research, or science; strong desire to learn new things; be valued for intellectual prowess
Leadership – make a significant difference for achieving shared goals; have impact
Learning – acquiring new, modifying, or synthesizing existing knowledge, behaviors, skills, values, or preferences; detecting and correcting errors
Legacy - directing resources (time, talent, money) to causes you care about in order to make a significant difference in the world that continues even after you are gone
Leisure - time without obligations or work responsibilities, and therefore being free to engage in enjoyable activities
Liberalism – belief in the importance of liberty and equal rights, generally pro progress or reform in political or religious affairs
Love – intense feelings of tender affection and compassion for others
Loyalty – supporting a person or cause due to your feelings/attitude of devoted attachment and affection through challenging as well as good times

Making a difference - leaving the world a better place for having lived; having a significant impact in your sphere of influence	
Mastery – possession of consummate skill, control, command, or grasp or a skill, ability, or organization, or people; having the upper hand in a contest/competition	
Materialism - acquiring and protecting wealth or objects are desirable; material possessions are a sign of success	
Membership – a sense of belonging and therefore contributing your time, talents, skills, and energy to organizations, clubs, and institutions	
Multiculturalism – appreciation, acceptance, and promotion of multiple cultures	
Natural abilities (use) – use innate gifts as way to acknowledge life purpose	
Naturalness – be able to dress and be casual, your natural self	
Nature – being concerned with animals, environment and people's impact on nature; being outdoors	
New ideas – appreciation of new concepts, approaches, theories, inventions, etc.	
Objectivity – approach people, tasks, or decisions with detachment, appreciation for cause and effect, neutrality, and accuracy	
Opportunity – a condition of openness such that every one has access to resources necessary for a fulfilling life	
Order – a condition of logical, methodical, and comprehensible arrangement among separate elements, processes, or people in a group	
Organizing – the act of rearranging or coordinating people, processes, objects, events, or elements	
Parenting - to have, acquire, and use experiences, skills, and responsibilities involved in teaching and caring for children	
Past - tradition and history are important and provide guidelines for living life	
Patriotism - pride in or devotion to your country	
Peace – mental calm and serenity, without anxiety, making sure you and others get along without war, conflict, fights	
People – interest in, value of, concern for well-being of other human beings	
People (contact) – have frequent, quality interaction with others	
Perfection – complete flawlessness, free from fault or defect, the highest degree of proficiency, skill or excellence	

	Personal control – expecting to control your life and environment to sustain or improve your quality of life
	Physical activity – be able to have energetic movement or exercise
	Physical challenge – perform activities, sports, stunts, etc., that require hard labor, pit you against others physically, or test your own physical limits
	Place/space – be in surroundings that reflect your lifestyle, preferences, values, and interests
	Power - the capacity to influence the behavior of others to achieve a result and to have impact; the right, authority, or desire to have power-over or power-with others
	Practicality – action orientation with sensible, hands-on approach to work
	Pragmatism – linking of practice with theory; practical approach to problems and affairs that balances ideals with what works
	Precision – work/live in ways where there is little room for error
	Progress – positive movement toward a goal or something valued; growth, development, advancement
	Preservation – guarding children, nature, people, animals, or things from danger, harm, or injury
	Quality – excellent standard or level of service, product, action, event, etc.
	Quest (spirituality) – honestly facing existential questions in their complexity (e.g., Why are we here? Why is there death? What is the purpose of life? why earth-humans-animals? etc.), while at the same time resisting clear-cut, pat answers
	Reality – the state of things as they actually exist, rather than as they might appear or be imagined; authenticity
	Reciprocity – relationships involve mutual exchange of obligations, favors, and privileges
	Recognition – receive validation and acknowledgment from others for your effort-based accomplishments
	Relationships – have time to develop and maintain quality contact with people you care about
	Respect – admiration and acknowledgment from others; wanting others to admire and defer to you
	Responsibility – willingness to be accountable for your charges in life

Results – see bottom-line, measurable, tangible impact of your actions and work
Retirement - leaving a job or career; the end of the time when you work for money
Ritual – a set of actions performed regularly, often with an unchanging pattern
Self-discipline - practicing methods that ensure controlled and orderly behavior; mental self-control used to direct or change behavior or learn something
Self expression – sharing your personality, feelings, or ideas through work, speech, art, life
Self-help - initiative, hard work, and individual accomplishment are essential qualities
Service – give support, information, and advice to others
Shared values – be with others who agree with you about what is most important in life and how to reach mutual goals
Simplicity – a straightforward quality of life without complications, difficulties, or embellishments
Spirituality - growth and introspection are seen as the purpose of life and the measure of one's worth
Solitude – a state of being alone, remote or secluded
Stability/Security – regular, predictable work-life through the use of routines and structure with predictable income
Status – have or earn prestige with a reputation based on achievements, talents, skills, or family; have a positive public image
Supervising – oversee people and activities, usually in a work arena
Surrender - to release; to let go; to relinquish possession or control to somebody (something, e.g., God/fate) greater than yourself (your ego)
Talents (use) – use innate aptitudes, flair, gifts, abilities, or capacities
Task accomplishment – carry out projects in a systematic way to meet goals, output, or performance objectives
Time: alone - spending time in solitude, separated from other people; usually in quiet, remote, or secluded places where human activity is limited or absent
Time: cyclical - importance attached to doing things in season
Time: linear - importance attached to schedules, calendars, deadlines, watches, and being "on time"

	Time: procedural - doing things when everything comes together naturally
	Tradition - heritage, continuity, and stability are desired and worth continuing
	Transformation – change involving an end to some aspect of self you valued and becoming something new
	Travel - to journey to and visit different people, cultures, and places in the world
	Trust – the ability to have confidence in, and reliance on, others' goodwill in situations involving risk or interdependence
	Utilitarianism – the proper course of action is one that is useful and maximizes the greatest good; the value of something is determined by its usefulness
	Wealth – have, gain, or maintain a high economic standard of living; high net worth
	Well-defined responsibilities – use training, skills, abilities, and experience to do clearly defined tasks with delineated roles and expectations
	Winning – achieving victory or success by defeating an opponent; gaining something of value through skill and or luck
	Wisdom - the knowledge and experience needed to make sensible, caring decisions and judgments
	YOUR VALUES AND YOUR DEFINTIONS Use the spaces below to add values not included in the inventory.

Step 2. If you did not already do so, go back to **WORKSHEET #2** and write out *your definition* of each of your top five values. You may use the definitions provided on the VALUES INVENTORY. But since these are your values, it is helpful for you to define each value in the way that is most meaningful for you. I strongly encourage you to actually write your values on **WORKSHEET #2** by hand for this first time. You can type them in later. Connecting physically to what is meaningful for you tends to make a positive difference for people.

Did you know?

While values and priorities differ substantially from person to person, and culture to culture, five values are shared widely among people around the world. These are
honesty,
respect,
responsibility,
fairness, and
compassion.
The specifics of how we understand and enact those values may vary by person and by culture – but those basic values tend to connect us all as human beings.

WORKSHEET #3: Values Clarification Grid

In this exercise you will differentiate espoused (talked about) values from enacted (lived) values. You will also share your top five values with at least one other person. List your top five values in the first column from the left, and then follow the instructions that start on the next page.

YOUR TOP 5 VALUES	✓	✓	✓	✓	✓
1					
2					
3					
4					
5					

Values Clarification Step 1: In the second column next to each of your values, put a check mark if you are proud of that value.

Values Clarification Step 2: In the third column next to each of your values, put a check mark if you have told at least one person, out loud, that this is one of your values. If you have publicly affirmed that value, put a check mark next to each of the five values.

Values Clarification Step 3: In the fourth column next to each of your values, put a check mark next to that value if you have chosen that value. Have you considered the alternative to that value? Have you considered the pros? The cons? The consequences of living according to that value? Have you freely chosen that value. Many people have absorbed their values from their families, community, the media - and not truly chosen their values. We often don't even know what our values are until we've encountered someone with different values. So only put check marks next to values where you're certain you have chosen your value freely.

Remember, the list of values you used to select your top five values includes a lot of values that might be positive alternatives to yours. In that way it is a good resource for you.

Values Clarification Step 4: In the fifth column next to each of your values, put a check mark next to each of your five values if you can remember a time and can tell another person of a time that you have acted, at least once, on that value.

Values Clarification Step 5: In this final column, put a check mark next to the value if you act consistently on this value. People know you walk your talk when it comes to this value. People know that your behavior is predictable, consistent and trustworthy when it comes to this value.

Now if you have any empty boxes in your grid, you have an opportunity for action. When you are looking at projects, entrepreneurial opportunities, or jobs - be sure to check that opportunity with your top values.

If you reflect for a while and then revisit the values inventory, you may discover that when it comes to your actions (what you do) vs. your thoughts about what you *should* do, you enact some different core values. You then have a choice. You can change your core values to more accurately reflect your enacted values, or you might decide to act more consistently in alignment with your values.

WORKSHEET #4: Voicing Values

One way to start living according to your values is to voice your values out loud with another person. Values researcher Mary C. Gentile[1] found that by voicing your values and stating your intent to live according to those values, you are less likely to get confused when you are in situations that call for you to act according to those values. Use the values and definitions you prepared on the Values Worksheet #2. And be prepared to share what you have written with another person out loud.

1 I value _____ and this means _____
_____
_____

I am proud of my _____ value.

I intend to act in ways consistent with my _____ value.

2 I value _____ and this means _____
_____
_____

I am proud of my _____ value.

I intend to act in ways consistent with my _____ value.

3 I value _____ and this means _____
_____
_____

I am proud of my _____ value.

I intend to act in ways consistent with my _____ value.

4 I value _____ and this means _____
_____
_____

I am proud of my _____ value.

I intend to act in ways consistent with my _____ value.

5 I value _____ and this means _____
_____
_____

I am proud of my _____ value.

I intend to act in ways consistent with my _____ value.

WORKSHEET #5a: Work Values

In addition to your top five life values, there are values that make a positive difference in your work experience. On the next two pages you will identify those values. These are the same values included in the VALUES INVENTORY, this time without all the definitions.

Step 1: Highlight your top five values.

Step 2: Put an *X* in column 1 next to any activity-related value you need to do.

Step 3: Put an *X* in column 2 next to any value you need to have in your work or life to be happy.

Step 4: Put an *X* in column 3 for any value that must be in your environment for you to be satisfied.

There is no limit here to the number of X's you can use, but the more you focus on what is *truly* important to you, the more useful this worksheet will be for you

VALUE	1	2	3
Acceptance			
Access			
Accuracy			
Achievement			
Advancement			
Adventure			
Aging well			
Altruism			
Artistic expression			
Authority			
Autonomy			
Beauty/aesthetics			
Being			
Birthright			
Challenge			
Change			
Charity			
Cleanliness			
Comfort			
Commitment			
Communication			
Community			
Compassion			

VALUE	1	2	3
Competence			
Competition			
Conservation			
Conservatism			
Context/place			
Contribution			
Cosmopolitan			
Courage			
Creativity			
Curiosity			
Democracy			
Detail			
Dignity			
Direct communication			
Discipline			
Discovery			
Diversity			
Doing/activity			
Duty			
Empathy			
Empiricism			
Equality/egalitarianism			
Excellence			

VALUE	1	2	3
Expertise			
Expressiveness			
Extraversion			
Extrinsic religiosity			
Fairness			
Faith			
Family			
Fate			
Financial freedom			
Formality			
Freedom			
Friendship			
Fundamentalism			
Future			
Generosity			
Group/collectivism			
Growth			
Harmony			
Healing			
Help others			
Hierarchy			
Honesty			
Human interaction			
Humility			
Idealism			
Immanence spirituality			
Independence			
Indirect communication			
Individuality			
Influence			
Informality			
Initiative			
Innovation			
Integrity			
Intellectual challenge			
Introversion			
Intrinsic religiosity			
Joy			
Justice			
Kindness			
Knowledge/expertise			
Leadership			

VALUE	1	2	3
Learning			
Legacy			
Leisure			
Liberalism			
Love			
Loyalty			
Making a difference			
Mastery			
Materialism			
Membership			
Multiculturalism			
Natural ability			
Naturalness			
Nature			
New ideas			
Objectivity			
Opportunity			
Order			
Organizing			
Parenting			
Past			
Patriotism			
Peace			
People			
People contact			
Perfection			
Personal control			
Physical activity			
Physical challenge			
Place/space			
Power			
Practicality			
Pragmatism			
Precision			
Progress			
Preservation			
Quality			
Quest spirituality			
Reality			
Reciprocity			
Recognition			
Relationships			

VALUE	1	2	3
Respect			
Responsibility			
Results			
Retirement			
Ritual			
Self-discipline			
Self-expression			
Self-help			
Service			
Shared values			
Simplicity			
Spirituality			
Solitude			
Stability/security			
Status			
Supervising			
Surrender			
Talents			
Task accomplishment			
Time alone			

Time: cyclical			
Time: linear			
Time: procedural			
Tradition			
Transformation			
Travel			
Trust			
Utilitarianism			
Wealth			
Well-defined responsibilities			
Winning			
Wisdom			

OTHER VALUES

WORKSHEET #5b: Team Values

This 15-item worksheet helps you identify values that influence the ways you work with others on teams. Making team values apparent helps you manage differences and team conflict

Instructions: Circle the number (between 1 and 7) that most closely represents your value. For example, if you are very formal, circle number 1; if you are very informal, circle number 7; if you have no preference for formality or informality, circle number 4, and so on.

	VALUE		VALUE
1	Formal	1 2 3 4 5 6 7	Informal
2	Listening	1 2 3 4 5 6 7	Talking
3	Structured	1 2 3 4 5 6 7	Flexible
4	Tradition	1 2 3 4 5 6 7	Change
5	Collaboration	1 2 3 4 5 6 7	Competition
6	What you know	1 2 3 4 5 6 7	Who you know
7	Task	1 2 3 4 5 6 7	Relationship
8	Fixed rules	1 2 3 4 5 6 7	No rules
9	Harmony (by avoiding issues)	1 2 3 4 5 6 7	Harmony (by confronting issues)
10	Customer first	1 2 3 4 5 6 7	Company first
11	Team	1 2 3 4 5 6 7	Individual
12	Security	1 2 3 4 5 6 7	Risk
13	Hierarchy	1 2 3 4 5 6 7	Equity
14	Quality	1 2 3 4 5 6 7	Quantity
15	Long-term goals	1 2 3 4 5 6 7	Short-term goals

Share your team values with others on your work teams.

Values clarification is an important and lifelong activity. The exercises you did here in this part of the workbook will provide a good foundation.

CAREER BY DESIGN TOOL #1: Mission Statement

Crafting and memorizing your personal mission statement helps you remember your top five values and make decisions consistent with those values. For example, my personal mission statement is ...

I am happy, healthy, and peaceful being with people I love, in a place I love, doing creative and expressive work I love, all with financial freedom.

There are several elements to this mission statement.

- This mission statement includes my core values using words that resonate with me. I know that *happy*, *healthy*, and *peaceful* are states of being I value no matter what I am doing.

- I also find I have much more energy when I love something or someone. Energetically, I run more on love than on fear, challenge, or competition.

- I value working with people who are my friends, whom I trust, whom I care about and who care about me. I spend a lot of hours working, and those relationships matter as much to me as my big R relationships with family. And I value being near and with family members.

- I did not realize that *place* was an important value until I lived and worked in rainy, gray, cold, dreary, isolated places. I now admit to being solar-powered (I live in the desert) and seek physical spaces that are aesthetically pleasing to me. I also value living, working, and being in communities that are multicultural and inclusive. So the value *place* captures all of that for me.

- For many years my work was quantitative (I am a recovering finance professional), and data-research driven, in part because I put away my more creative–expressive side to find work that would bring me money, status, and approval. I also had an internal fear that "artists starve." So I did not choose to be creative and expressive although both of those attributes are part of my personality, nature, and talent base. After I started the *Career by Design* process, I reclaimed those aspects of self and reaffirmed them as core personal and professional values.

- I knew that I cared about money, but like many people in the United States, I was also ambivalent about holding money as a value. Only you can sort out what your feelings, thoughts, and beliefs truly are about money. With work and time, I came to know that what I truly valued was enough money to feel free to make decisions and live my life according to my values. Some people truly want wealth—and they know what that is. Others do not care too much about money at all. But for most of us, money represents, or allows us to have, something of even greater value. For me, that was freedom. If you notice that you make life and work decisions that seem to compromise your values because you need money, dig a little deeper into your values to uncover what is really important about money for you.

- The phrasing of the mission statement is in the powerful, empowering, present tense. Use words such as "I am" or "I allow" or "I accept." Avoid "I want", "I will try", "I hope", "I wish", "If I'm lucky", "I have to", "I must", "I should", "I need", etc. Avoid negative, doubtful, questioning terms. Affirm your mission in the now.

- The values are in priority order.

Enough about my mission statement! Pull our your Values Worksheet #2 and start drafting your personal mission statement below.

Mission Statement Draft

_____

_____

_____

_____

_____

_____.

Mission Statement Refined

_____

_____

_____

_____

_____.

Once you decide to
LIVE according to your values,
your luck and your life will change.

NEEDS

You will only thrive at work if the environment suits your basic needs. When your basic needs are not met, your work is a source of stress.

The Psychological Contract

There are many explicit expectations in the employer–employee relationship, such as salary, compensation, and job duties. In addition to the explicit agreements between employer and employees, there are often implicit, unacknowledged, and unspoken needs and expectations. These are part of the psychological contract. *The psychological contract is set of needs and expectations between you and another person, your teammates, or your organization. It influences what you expect from the key people in your life, as well as what employers expect from employees and what employees expect from employers.*

For the purpose of *Career by Design*, my focus is on psychological contracts in the workplace. In practice, at work, most psychological contracts are between managers and their direct reports. But you have relational needs that must be met in all kinds of social interactions. It should be emphasized that you need not communicate about, or agree on, the specifics of a psychological contract for the contract to exist *and* to have behavioral consequences. The psychological contract has an impact on the amount and quality of your relationships at work whether you can articulate them or not, whether your circumstance meets your needs or not.

However, many people do not communicate their needs and expectations clearly, to the appropriate person, or at the most effective times. Broken psychological contracts between people at work are at the root of many workplace conflicts, absenteeism, poor performance, career dissatisfaction, demotivation, stress, and costly employee turnover. Many researchers into job dissatisfaction and conflict believe that silence about the relational needs at work seems to be the rule, rather than the exception.

So why do we not communicate our work expectations with each other? First, we often do not even know what our needs are until we have been disappointed because some important need is not met. Second, the opportunity to actually discuss relational needs at work is relatively new. Until recently workers did mostly what they were told to do, and they were expected to keep their jobs until they retired unless they failed to perform in some important ways.

But times have changed. In today's workplace it is important to know what our needs are. *Needs motivate behavior.* Unmet needs cause stress and contribute to conflict. With greater empowerment of workers, especially in the service sectors, making sure that people are engaged, competent, and committed is important. With globalization and high-speed service delivery, interruptions in work flow due to unproductive conflict is costly. And for our purposes, knowing and communicating your needs empowers you to design a career that satisfies you.

The Birkman Method

The Birkman Method is a personality, social perception, and occupational interest assessment that will help you identify your behavioral styles, motivations, expectations, and stress behaviors. The Birkman also identifies your Usual behaviors that help you manage in your social circle and adapt to your surroundings. But the strength of the Birkman is delineating the gaps between what you do and what you need. *The Birkman is one of the best ways to gain insight into, and the language you need to articulate, negotiate, and take responsibility for getting your Needs met.*

Your needs are typically developed when you are between 7 and 9 years old, and they don't change much without major life events. These Needs are often hidden (even to self), so we use projective assessments, like the Birkman, to identify what those needs are. When your needs are met, life is good. And you demonstrate the effective, positive aspect of the Usual behavior described by the Birkman. If your Needs are not met, you are likely to demonstrate the stress-induced, reactive, and dysfunctional behavior also described by the Birkman.

The Birkman Reports are particularly valuable for actual and aspiring managers in business environments because they are used most often with that population. The full Birkman report can be expensive, and interpreting it without the assistance of a certified Birkman coach can be challenging. But there are a three Birkman reports that are more affordable and accessible even if you are just starting your career explorations: The Birkman Preview, the Profile Summary, and the Birkman-On-Demand report. These affordable Birkman reports can give you valuable insight for your Career by Design.

The Birkman on Demand report will give you text describing your unique ways of
- Being
- Being ineffective (your flaws)
- Being motivated
- Communicating
- Learning
- Managing and Leading
- Relating to others
- Working with others on teams - trust, conflict, commitment and accountability

The Birkman Profile Summary gives your scores for your relational components and needs but must be interpreted by a certified Birkman Coach. The Birkman Preview describes your relational strengths, needs, and stress behaviors plus it gives you a Career Report with active links for occupations suiting your needs.

To give you a sample of what the Birkman method profile says about needs, circle the items in the chart below if you feel you need the type of work environment described. If you find you do not have a strong preference for one side or the other, do not circle either side on that row. If you circle something, keep it in mind when you are designing your career.

Specific goals with praise and recognition for successes, public approval, a positive reputation	*Challenge*	Challenging work, stretch goals, and opportunities to prove yourself
Frank, direct, candid relationships and feedback	*esteem*	Respect for your title, status symbols, and approval from people you respect above you
Individualized goals, time to work alone, few meetings, contact with a few close friends	*acceptance*	Interactions with lots of people, appreciation for your social status, team work, reassurance
Minimal routine, informal work relationships, task-work variety	*structure*	Clear rules, systems, procedures, instructions and roles, predictable steady income
Autonomy, pleasant work relationships, input before decisions, suggestions vs. orders	*authority*	Enforced, firm, clear direction, ability to direct and debate with others
Service, harmony, teamwork, work more for service & the team than for money	*advantage*	Immediate, clear, personal benefits to you for success, compensation for performance
Intellectual and emotional engagement, recharge time, set own pace, low stress	*activity*	Practical results, competitive outlets in work or active hobbies, physical activities
Logical solutions, matter of fact interactions, concrete, clear instructions, practical tasks	*empathy*	Quality work relationships, opportunities to express your feelings, sustained relationships
Time and a chance to give your input before change is started, uninterrupted time, space	*change*	Task variety, changing-non-routine work, shift priorities as new interests arise
Predictability, routine, familiar-established rules and procedures, order, consistency	*freedom*	Independence, free action & thought, control over your schedule and your work, autonomy
A short time from when you make a decision to action, freedom to act, clarity, short meetings	*thought*	Time and space to think about options before acting, time to talk and hear others' perspectives

The Birkman Reports can also describe how your needs combine and provide even deeper insight into your needs when relating to others.

1. For example, if you need *Autonomy, pleasant work relationships, input before decisions, suggestions vs. orders* AND *Independence, free action and thought, control over your schedule and your work, autonomy,* THEN when it comes to conflict, you need opportunities to take independent action without debate, freedom from interference, low-key team interactions, and to work with team members who take initiative and take care of their own responsibilities.

2. If you need *Enforced, firm, clear direction, ability to direct and debate with others* AND *Predictability, routine, familiar-established rules and procedures, order, consistency,* THEN you need cooperation from others as well as input from them, opportunities to discuss options fully with team members, and a team that works together without suppressing differences or pushing one opinion.

These are different relational styles based on different needs. We often expect other people to know what we need without being conscious of our needs ourselves.

Use either your Birkman report or the chart above to clarify your work relationship needs. And after doing that, be sure to:

1. Prioritize the needs.
2. Decide whether or not your needs are being met, if you are evaluating your current work situation; whether or not your needs are likely to be met if you are evaluating a future situation.
3. Decide who is the person (or people) most likely to be able to help you meet your needs.
4. If the need is being met, tell that person, as a way to reinforce the situation, that you wish to see a continuation of behaviors that meet your needs. If the need is not being met, communicate your expectations to that person and together consider ways your needs and expectations could be met.
5. Agree on some behaviors that would help you meet your needs.

If you do not believe your needs can ever be met in that situation:

1. Discuss the need anyway (give people a chance before giving up on them).
2. Determine if you can live with that situation.
3. Gather more information about how meeting your needs could make the team or organization more effective, reduce conflict, or improve your relationship. *Or*
4. Modify your expectations.

Additional information about how needs motivate behavior is included at the end of this workbook in the Appendix: Needs and Motivation.

CHAPTER 4 - MOTIVATING INTERESTS

Motivating interests include . . .
- Those areas of work that attract you naturally
- The endeavors to which you bring the most passion
- Activities where work will seem like play for pay
- The best guide to the work content you enjoy
- The primary driver of career satisfaction over your lifetime

The underlying patterns of our motivating interests, even our work interests, start when we are young and stay with us throughout our lifetimes.

In this chapter you do a number of activities.

WORKSHEET #6: Motivating Interests—20 Things You Love to Do

In this exercise you will identify activities you love to do from childhood to the present. These activities need not be work related. The exercise requires you to follow a process that you will have live (in a workshop) or by following the audio instructions.

WORKSHEET #7: Top 10 Motivating Interests

In this exercise you will use the INTEREST INVENTORY to identify your top 10 interests, your degree of interest, specifics associated with those interests, and skills you use when pursuing those interests.

After completing your Top 10 Motivating Interests I have provided questions in the **Interests Inventory Reflection** section that guide your inquiry into why those interests motivate you and themes those interests may represent. In the subsection on **Interest Themes**, I describe seven common interest themes with some characteristics people with those interest themes often share.

The supporting **Interests Resources** I recommend at the end of this chapter for deeper exploration into motivating interests are the MBTI-based book *Do What You Are*, the Strong Inventory, and a couple of Birkman reports.

WORKSHEET #6: Motivating Interests—20 Things You Love to Do

star	new	plan	A/O	$, €	#	20 Things You Love to Do
					1	
					2	
					3	
					4	
					5	
					6	
					7	
					8	
					9	
					10	
					11	
					12	
					13	
					14	
					15	
					16	
					17	
					18	
					19	
					20	

Instructions for 20 Things You Love to Do

Step 1. Write a list of 20 things in life you love to do to the right of the numbers on the worksheet. It doesn't matter if you do it well. These do not have to be work or career related. In fact I'd like you to stay open minded and think of ALL kinds of things you love to do. You know you love to do it when you lose track of time, you're just in joy, in flow. These can be things from the past, when you were a child, from now, that you imagine for the future. And because this is a private activity, you don't have to censor yourself in any way.

> *Here are some examples just in case you need a memory jog. Maybe you like music, art, painting, museums, walks on the beach, in the woods, singing, dancing, playing games, sports - watching, doing, playing, organizing, drawing, reading, taking things apart, putting things together, telling people what to do, eating, going out, shopping, being with kids, with animals, pets, talking, acting, speeches, telephone, writing, theater, dancing, playing computer games, driving, decorating, looking at houses, etc.*

Step 2: To the left of each numbered item,
Put a money sign to the left of the item if it costs more than $10 (or 10 Euros, 10 Lira, etc.) each time you do it.

> *Sometimes what we love doing costs a lot of money. If that's the case then we need to have, or make a lot of money to be happy. In many cases, however, the things we love to do are not expensive. What they require is that we make TIME and space in our lives to do them.*

Step 3: Place an "A" to the left of the item if you prefer to do that activity "Alone"; "O" if with other people; leave blank if either alone or with others.

> *If you have lots of A's - for Alone, then you are likely very contained and have a strong inner world. In the Myers Briggs typology you might be an introvert, a person energized through their own inner world of ideas, interacting with objects by themselves, or with one-on-one conversations with people they really know and trust. Again, the challenge here is to make space and time to do what you love in a culture that is highly extraverted and expects you to get out their and do stuff with other people. If you have lots of "O's" then you enjoy doing things with others. The challenge for you will be figuring out how to do what you love when others are not available to do the things you love to do with you.*

Step 4: Put a "P" next to each item if requires planning on your part. You decide what's planning for you. Planning may be an hour or so for some people, for others planning might mean weeks or months. The point is to notice what comes up for you. If you're more spontaneous in doing what you love, or need to make time to do what you love.

Step 5: Put "N" for "new interest" next to items that would not have been there 5 years ago.

Many adults have things they've loved to do since they were young. Their motivating interests started when they were young, and continue throughout their lives. Especially when they think of why they enjoy doing something, they see certain themes emerging. On the other hand, if you're a person with lots of N's - then you're a bit of an explorer, open to change, and trying new things. That's also an insight. It's not just the content of the things you love to do, but the excitement and joy you get from trying, learning, or doing something new.

Step 6: Select 3-5 items and *(star) them if they are extremely enjoyable for you.

Step 7: Now reflect.

What themes emerge when you think of the the things you love to do?

What is it about these activities that is energizing for you?

Why do you enjoy doing the types of things you listed?

Look at your list of things you love to do again. When is the last time you did them?

Step 8. Look at your list of things you love to do again, especially the starred items. What will it take for you to do that activity in the next month?

Step 9. Make a commitment to add at least those 3 things you love to do to your work life or leisure activities. Write that commitment down and share it with another person. Schedule it if you must. Make an appointment with yourself. Then do it.

INTEREST INVENTORY

Step 1: *Identify Motivating Interests.* Find your top 10 motivating interests in the list below. A motivating interest energizes you. Go through the list quickly and rate your degree of interest in that activity. Give the interest a 10 rating if when you're doing it, you go into a zone, lose track of time, and life is good. Rate it lower, say a 9, if it is not quite as interesting to you. If you need to do so, go down to 8's in order to find your top 10 interests.

Interest	Rating	Interest	Rating
A particular place		Audiovisual equipment	
A particular time		Banking	
Accounting		Big business/corporations	
Acting/performing		Biology	
Action/activity		Bookkeeping	
Adapting		Brainstorming	
Adjusting to changing tasks		Bringing people together	
Administration		Budgeting	
Adventure		Building things	
Advising		Campaign management	
Advocacy		Caring for others	
Aeronautics, space		Cartooning, Magna, Illustration	
Airplanes		Cause–effect analysis	
Analysis		Celebrating shared achievement	
Animals		Championing people, ideas	
Anthropology		Change management	
Archeology		Classifying data, information	
Architecture		Clerical activities	
Architecture		Coaching	
Art		Coalition building	
Asking questions		Collaborating	
Assessing people		Commanding	

Interest	Rating
Communicating expectations	
Communicating graphically	
Communicating in writing	
Communicating verbally	
Communicating visually	
Competing	
Composing	
Computer games	
Computer graphics, animation	
Conflict management	
Confronting people	
Connecting people	
Construction/building	
Consulting	
Convincing	
Cooking	
Coordinating people, info	
Counseling	
Crafts	
Creativity	
Criminology	
Critiquing	
Cross-cultural experiences	
Cruising high seas	
Cultural competence	
Customer service	
Dance	

Interest	Rating
Data processing	
Death, dying, hospice	
Debating	
Decorating	
Delegating	
Demonstrating	
Design	
Details	
Developing others	
Diagnoses	
Directing	
Directing others	
Disclosing	
Discovering things	
Discussing the meaning of life	
Displaying	
Diversity/multiculturalism	
Doing a sport or athletic activity	
Doing skilled work with hands	
Drawing	
Ecology	
Economics	
Editing	
Editorializing	
Education	
Electronics	
Encouraging	

Interest	Rating
Endurance activities/sports	
Energizing	
Engineering	
Entertaining	
Entrepreneurship	
Environmental issues	
Evaluating	
Examining things, ideas	
Explaining key issues	
Exploration	
Exploring new ideas	
Expressing confidence	
Expressing ideas through arts	
Facilitating groups	
Fact finding	
Farming	
Filing	
Film, film making	
Financial analysis	
Financial service	
Following through, up	
Food service, restaurants	
Forecasting, projections	
Foreign languages	
Fundraising	
Games	
Gardening	

Interest	Rating
Genealogy	
Giving clear, engaging direction	
Giving credit for ideas	
Giving feedback	
Goal setting	
Government	
Graphics	
Growing plants	
Health	
Helping others	
High-stress activities	
Hiring good people	
History	
Home	
Human resources	
Humanities	
Humor	
Hypothetical exploration	
Idea generation	
Identifying problems	
Imagining, visioning	
Implementing tasks, projects	
Improving things	
Influencing others	
Innovation	
Innovation management	
Inspecting	

Interest	Rating
Installing equipment	
Insurance	
Insurance	
Integrating different ideas	
Interpersonal interaction	
Interviewing	
Intuition	
Invention	
Inventorying	
Investigating	
Investments	
Jokes, Comedy	
Law	
Law enforcement	
Leadership	
Leading	
Learning	
Listening	
Literature	
Logistics	
Machines	
Making a profit	
Making decisions	
Making judgment calls	
Management	
Managing	
Managing conflict	

Interest	Rating
Managing diversity	
Managing operations	
Managing people	
Managing resources	
Managing stress	
Manufacturing/making things	
Maps	
Marketing (advertising, sales)	
Measuring work	
Mechanics	
Media (TV, radio, Internet)	
Medicine	
Mentoring	
Military	
Money	
Monitoring	
Motivating others	
Motivating yourself	
Music	
Nature	
Negotiating	
Networking	
Oceans	
Officiating, refereeing	
Oil rigs/exploration	
Operating equipment	
Organizing people, ideas, info	

Interest	Rating
Outdoors	
Overseeing	
Owning your own business	
Painting	
Painting, drawing, cartooning	
Parks & rec	
Patience with process	
Peace	
Performance evaluations	
Performing arts	
Personal growth	
Perspective taking	
Persuading people	
Philanthropy	
Photography	
Physical activity	
Physical fitness	
Planning	
Planning events parties	
Playing a musical instrument	
Poetry	
Policy making	
Politics (savvy)	
Presenting	
Print	
Priority setting	
Process management	

Interest	Rating
Producing	
Production management	
Promoting	
Protecting	
Providing helpful information	
Public relations	
Public speaking	
Publishing	
Racing	
Raising children, animals, plants	
Raising money	
Reading	
Real Estate	
Receiving feedback	
Reconciling	
Recording	
Recreation/leisure	
Reflecting	
Relationships	
Religion/spirituality	
Repairing things	
Research	
Resource preservation	
Respecting others	
Risk taking	
Romance	
Sailing	

Interest	Rating
Scheduling	
Science	
Seeking different perspectives	
Selling	
Service	
Serving people	
Setting goals	
Setting priorities	
Sharing information	
Sharing power	
Shopping	
Socializing	
Software design	
Solving problems	
Solving puzzles	
Sporting events	
Sports	
Strategy	
Statistics/mathematics	
Staying the course	
Storytelling	
Strategic planning	
Stress management	
Structure	
Studying things, people, animals	
Synthesizing	
Taking a stand	

Interest	Rating
Taking risks	
Talking	
Teaching	
Team building	
Team work	
Technical learning	
Technology	
Technology	
Tending animals	
Therapy, psychology	
Time management	
Tools	
Training	
Transcribing	
Translation	
Travel	
Trusting people	
Understanding	
Understanding feelings	
Unions	
Updating	
Using your expertise	
Variety	
Visioning the future	
Visual arts	
Win–win negotiating	
Work–life balance	

Interest	Rating
Working with data	
Working with ideas	
Working with numbers	
Working with people	
Working with technical info	

Interest	Rating
Working with the land	
Working with things	
Working with your hands	
Writing	
Writing songs, slogans, jingles	

WORKSHEET #7: Top 10 Motivating Interests

TOP 10 INTERESTS	Rating	Specifics and Associated Skills
1		
2		
3		
4		
5		
6		
7		
8		
9		
10		

Step 3: Interest Inventory Reflection

What themes do you notice as you look at your interests?

Why are you attracted to and motivated by these activities?

Which of your motivating interests are you using in your current work?

Which of your motivating interests are you using in leisure activities?

If you are not using your motivating interests in either your work or leisure activities, what ideas do you have for incorporating them into your life?

Motivating Interest Themes

When you examine your interests, you may gain insight not only into the content of the work you would like to do, but also into your personal work style and preferred work settings. In each of the theme descriptions below, I describe some common characteristics of people who are motivated by the key themes share. The seven themes are people, things, creativity, research, numbers/data, nature, and sports/activity. These themes put motivating interests into context. I describe some of the attractive qualities of each theme and some common challenges people with that theme may have to overcome.

Theme: People

Working with other people often means you are attracted to work where you can have frequent interactions (preferably face-to-face), and where you share similar values to your colleagues. You probably want time to develop yourself, and you appreciate organizations that support professional development of employees. You will grow by learning to manage conflict effectively and understanding that sometimes businesses make tough decisions to keep the business profitable, not just keeping the people happy. And you should learn to balance professional requirements with your personal needs.

A note on working with people

Most of us work with other people, even when working with people is not a core theme. It is therefore helpful to think about and decide what kind of relationship you want when working with others. Here are some different ways you may want to work with people.

-

- Leadership: Perhaps you want to influence others to take actions you believe will be best for achieving a shared goal. Perhaps you enjoy telling people what to do. You are willing to push and direct people in directions that you believe are right and efficient. This kind of relationship is one of *power-over* others.

- Autonomy: You may prefer to use your own initiative in your work, without significant guidance or direction from any other person. You may be a self-starter who dislikes (even occasionally resents) any interference when you are doing your work. You may be somewhat anti-authoritarian and resist any one trying to control you, your actions, or your output. You might think of this as being *individually empowered*.

- Collaboration: You may prefer to work with others on an equal playing field. You really enjoy the interaction and camaraderie that comes with teamwork. This is a *power-with* relationship.

- Service: You may want to help others achieve their goals and objectives, make them feel better, or take care of them in some way. This can be thought of as *empowering others*.

It is possible to combine these too. For instance you might have a combination of Service–Leadership, such as a minister; Collaboration–Leadership, such as a team leader; or Autonomy–Collaboration, such as being a key member of a product design team.

Theme: Things

If you really enjoy working with things, you may also appreciate manual dexterity and well-crafted products and tools. Perhaps you value precision—in thought and action. Do you like tangible, visible output? Working well with things often requires concentration, patience, pragmatism, and physical coordination—and as a person who enjoys working with things, you are likely to value similar qualities in your coworkers, leaders, and organizations. You like to be able to speak directly, to get to the point, to limit the small talk and unnecessary chit-chat at work, to focus on the task (not on relationships), to learn from past experience so you don't repeat mistakes in the present, to work alone, and to follow precise and predictable procedures to achieve high-quality output consistently. You may avoid presentations and social situations, brainstorming, and social niceties—these skills thus being opportunities for your personal and professional development.

Theme: Creativity

If you noticed a strong inclination to communicate through the arts—visual, verbal, craft, musical, performing—you may also find that you value individual expression, autonomy, and contributing to your work-world in your own unique way. Often people with a strong interest in the creative and expressive arts do not aim to be artists per se, but rather create their own unique lives without undue regard for the opinions of life's ever-present critics. You probably have a strong anti-authoritarian streak—not necessarily wanting to control other people but not wanted to be controlled by others either. Personal control over your life is very important to you. And you are willing to delegate routine, administrative, and repetitive tasks to others who seem to enjoy them more. Sometimes that's the budget—and not paying attention to those details can cost you—literally and politically. You are willing to come up with ingenious, original solutions to problems and may sometimes get bored doing the same old thing, over and over. Getting used to those aspects of work-life that are routine or require adherence to specific standards can help you become more effective at work in the long run. Learning to prioritize, manage your time, plan, and pay attention to the value of your contributions can move you forward in your career.

Theme: Research

Perhaps you are very interested in research, investigation, and analysis of information in order to discover the secrets of the universe, or life, or a product. You value knowledge—learning, sharing, using information that helps you develop ideas, drawing logical conclusions, using resources more wisely, being seen as an expert, or coming up with new theories. You enjoy the respect of your intellectual peers, explaining complex ideas, and making an intellectual contribution. Freedom means having time to explore your intellectual pursuits without being bothered by matters you consider trivial (matters unrelated to the ideas you are investigating at that time). The social niceties may not appeal much to you, nor political activities at work, nor talking to people who don't seem quite as intelligent as you are. Organizations are made up of all kinds of people; being able to simplify complex ideas to make them accessible and useful in your company, to understand the dynamics of politics and power at work, and to involve others in projects of value to you and your organization will be skills that serve you well as you grow in your career.

Theme: Numbers/Data

You may really have a knack for, and enjoyment of, working with numbers and data; loving the elegance, clarity, precision, order, reliability, and beauty of numbers (especially when compared to the messier interactions and ambiguity you encounter when dealing with people). The qualities you enjoy about numbers are probably metaphorically descriptive of the qualities you appreciate in your organization and its leaders. You may speak in a clear, quiet, precise, sequential manner in order to be accurate, efficient, and precise. Numbers and data coordinate, and you enjoy coordinating your efforts with other team members, using a structured approach in the service of clear goals. You probably prefer a more predictable, planned approach to change—if change is necessary at all. If you had your druthers, you'd work in an information-oriented, task-focused organization. Your attention to detail is legendary, yet sometimes you could pay more attention to the big picture, be open to exploration of new and different ways of doing things, get more comfortable with ambiguity and relational messiness, and recognize that other styles can also make an important contribution to overall organizational effectiveness. As you learn to develop those skills and appreciate stylistic diversity, you may find that your career success is greater.

Theme: Nature

If you love nature, you probably also believe that nature teaches many lessons, and not just about survival. You probably have a bias toward action—quick actions when necessary, slow action when it's better to slow down and smell the roses. Nature teaches us about its cycles—nurture, growth, harvest, death, regrowth—whether plants or animals. You are likely to be willing and able to understand the cycles and seasons of change, both metaphorically and literally. If your outdoors interests run toward growing things, then you are likely willing to plant and watch—an ability to give things time to come to fruition. You also know that the roots create the fruits and have a sense of how we reap what we sow. If you love being with and nurturing animals, you have a sense of the instinctive, pragmatic, and impersonal ways of the world. You know that sometimes it's not about you —and thoughts and feelings are nice, but things still have to be done, in season, on time. Your style is likely to be down-to-earth, with a preference for communicating more through your actions than your ideas.

Theme: Sports/Activity

If you have a strong interest in doing or watching sports, you may find that you also enjoy physicality and action in general, a clear beginning and end to tasks, goal-directed behavior, and focused, energetic activity. It's also likely that you like teamwork, a good challenge, negotiating, and the strong sense of accomplishment that comes from a job well done. With a preference for the now, the present, you might find it helpful in your career to do more long-term planning and strategic thinking accompanied by developing an appreciation for subtler forms of communication.

Additional Interest Resources

The themes mentioned here are a small number of the possible themes you might find when you combine your interests and reflect on *why* you enjoy those activities. There are a few additional resources I recommend for identifying interests.

The Strong Interest Inventory will provide you with suggested careers, courses, and activities you might do associated with your interests.

The Myers–Briggs Type Indicator (MBTI)–based book *Do What You Are* correlates your personality-based interests with hundreds of possible careers, and gives you strategies consistent with your personality for finding a satisfactory career. It is based on the observation that interests are often correlated with our personality profiles.

Both the Strong Interest Inventory and the MBTI are Consulting Psychologies Press (CPP) products and require a qualified administrator to provide you with access to them. You can find out even more about these tools by visiting the CPP site.

If you are a college student, these two assessments are usually available through your career center. If you are working with a coach, he or she probably can grant you access. And you can always contact me.

In addition to the needs information provided by the Birkman Method[2] mentioned in the "Values and Needs" chapter, the Birkman Method Career Report organizes your motivating interests into themes and links those interests to possible careers and to online resources about current occupational outlooks. The Birkman On Demand report will provide you with a prioritized list of possible careers and associated job duties using your specific needs and interests. You also get job search suggestions, information about how you approach interviews (both effective and ineffective behaviors), organizational fit, and a description of how your interests affect your work. Visit the Birkman site to find out more.

Although these resources can be helpful guides, many people need a special career niche, not found in these resources, to tap their unique combination of values, needs, personality, interests, talents, and skills. There are so many new career options, with the list changing rapidly, that you may not find your perfect career listed in any book or computer report. These resources help many people focus their attention. But if you do the exercises in this *Career by Design* workbook, and pay attention to what motivates you, I have no doubt of your eventual career success.

Interests Matter for Career Satisfaction

Do not underestimate the importance of identifying your career-related interests for having a successful career. Interests really matter. They signal the content of the work that will be most intrinsically energizing for you. By choosing work consistent with your interests, you are more likely to build a foundation of competence, credibility, and confidence early in your career. Doing work that is grounded in your core interests will sustain your efforts during those times when you are challenged or disappointed by other aspects of your work. I strongly urge everyone to choose work that they love—to play for pay. Your love of your work will make it so much easier to handle slow(er) promotions, biased performance reviews, or other work-related obstacles at various points in your career. Doing work you love and do well also means that you start on the right foot and build credibility and capital with your organization. And when it's all said and done, if you've loved the work all along, you will be able to say, I've had a life-affirming career. This choice is yours.

People who are happiest in their careers

PLAY for PAY!

Once you know your motivating interests, it is also important to combine those interests with your talents and strengths so that you have useful skills. Let's explore strengths and skills next.

CHAPTER 5 - STRENGTHS AND SKILLS

Career satisfaction and success come from doing what you love and doing what you do well. In order to have a career by design, you will therefore need to know what you do well —your strengths and skills.

This chapter provides a number of activities to help you identify your strengths and skills. First I introduce you to the strengths used by Gallup's StrengthFinders Inventory.

Then you use the *Career by Design* SKILLS INVENTORY and follow the instructions in this chapter to complete a number of worksheets:

WORKSHEET #8: Top 10 Skills
WORKSHEET #9: High Interest and Associated Skills
WORKSHEET #10: Skills I Need to Improve
WORKSHEET #11: Skills I Want to Improve

In addition to the skills listed in the SKILLS INVENTORY, I provide a list of RELATIONAL SKILLS that are useful for those of you who work with people to get things done. All too often people adept at using these skills undervalue the skills, or are undervalued because their importance and impact in organizations are invisible.

Accurate assessment of ability requires feedback; the Lominger VOICES 360 is my tool of choice for getting that feedback. I list the 67 competencies measured by that instrument and suggest other options for gaining feedback about your skill level.

If you are using *Career by Design* to guide career exploration, you may find the information about SkillScan, with its thematic organization and correlation of skills to possible occupations, very helpful at the end of this chapter.

STRENGTHS

Classic career coaching focuses on having people identify their skills and combine those skills with interests and values to suggest satisfying careers. More recently, the strengths-based approach, exemplified by the Gallup Organization's StrengthsFinders[3], has become popular, particularly with the two youngest generations in the workforce.

Based on Gallup's research, the best route to job satisfaction is to develop your top five strengths and to accumulate a track record for using those strengths to make a contribution in your career. Strengths are a combination of values, motivating interests, talents you may take for granted, and skills you do almost effortlessly. StrengthFinders Inventory cannot tell you how well you have actually developed those strengths. For that information it is best to get some type of feedback assessment.

Many people feel that the StrengthFinders Inventory tells you what makes you stand out. They say the list of action ideas is focused, practical, and helpful. The themes are:

1. **Achiever**—great deal of stamina, work hard, love to be busy and productive
2. **Activator**—make things happen, turn thoughts into action
3. **Adaptability**—go with the flow, now oriented
4. **Analytical**—search for reasons, causes, things that might affect a situation
5. **Arranger**—organize for maximum productivity
6. **Belief**—have unchanging core values with a defined purpose
7. **Command**—presence, charisma, take control and make decisions
8. **Communication**—find it easy to put thoughts into words
9. **Competition**—measure progress against performance of others, strive to win
10. **Connectedness**—faith in the links between all things, few coincidences, events have reasons
11. **Context**—enjoy thinking about the past as prologue to present
12. **Deliberative**—take serious care in making decisions and choices, anticipate obstacles
13. **Developer**—recognize and cultivate the potential in others
14. **Discipline**—enjoy routine, structure, order
15. **Empathy**—sense the feelings of others by imagining themselves in their lives/situations
16. **Fairness/consistency**—need to treat people fairly by setting up clear rules they use
17. **Focus**—can take a direction, follow through, correct, and stay on track; prioritize, then act
18. **Futuristic**—inspired by what could be and inspire others with their vision
19. **Harmony**—look for consensus and areas of agreement
20. **Ideation**—fascinated by ideas and able to find connections between seemingly disparate phenomena
21. **Includer**—accepting of others, aware when people feel left out and try to include them
22. **Individualization**—intrigued by the unique qualities of each person, with a gift for figuring out how people who are different can work together productively
23. **Input**—have a craving to know more, collect/archive all kinds of information
24. **Intellection**—introspective, actively intellectual, appreciate intellectual discussions
25. **Learner**—desire to learn and improve; the process of learning rather than outcome, excites them
26. **Maximizer**—focus on strengths as a way to stimulate personal and group excellence
27. **Positivity**—contagious enthusiasm, upbeat, get others excited
28. **Relator**—enjoy close relationships with others, find deep satisfaction in working hard with friends to achieve a goal
29. **Responsibility**—take psychological ownership of whatever they say and do; are committed to stable values such as honesty and loyalty
30. **Restorative**—adept at dealing with problems, figuring out what's wrong and dealing with it
31. **Self-assurance**—feel confident in their ability to manage their own lives
32. **Significance**—independent but want to be recognized as important by others
33. **Strategic**—faced with any given scenario, the spot patterns and issues quickly and create alternative ways to proceed
34. **WOO (Winning Others Over)**—love the challenge of meeting new people, winning them over, and making connections with other people

SKILLS

Skills are . . .

- Activities you do well.
- Competencies you have acquired.[4]
- Talents you have developed.

Usually you will develop a skill when you have been rewarded in some way for doing that activity. You might be rewarded in lots of different ways—by money, awards, promotions, approval, your own internal sense of accomplishment, positive feedback, and status. As a result you will keep doing what you are getting kudos for doing well, and become even better at doing those activities.

However, skills are not the primary indicator of career satisfaction, although you may feel really good about doing things well. According to research, skills are not as good a predictor of career effectiveness as are motivating interests.

But when you put motivating interests and skills together, your work-life is really good. Using the Career by Design ***Matrix in the next chapter, we will do just that.***

Skill assessment can be somewhat tricky because you want to do three things:
1. Get an accurate assessment of what skills you have
2. Know how skilled you are with the skills you have, and
3. Know what skills are most useful for the career you have, or wish to have.

The Skills Assessment on the next page will allow you to self-identify skills you believe you have. I will guide you through some questions that will help you gain a more objective assessment of whether you have used those skills productively. This is a good start for your skills assessment purpose #1.

For a more accurate assessment of your actual skill level (purpose #2), you will need additional information. To get that information you might:
*Consider your performance reviews.
*Ask for feedback from your colleagues.
*Do a 360 feedback assessment, such as the Lominger VOICES 360 Feedback report.

A coach can help you examine your reviews. To get organized, useful feedback from colleagues about how skilled you are, I suggest the Lominger VOICES 360 that I describe in more detail later in this chapter.

For the third purpose of a skills assessment—for example, to determine what skills you have or need for a particular job or career—I suggest SkillScan. In this workbook, I do not go into much detail for linking skills to specific jobs or careers, but I do describe SkillScan more near the end of this chapter.

Skills Inventory

Step 1. Select your top skills from the list on this page and the next. Because this list includes terms used in a number of skills and abilities assessments, some of the skills seem similar to others. If you do not find all of your top skills listed here, add the skill to **WORKSHEET #8 Top 10 Skills** using your own skill term. *Top skills* refers to those in which you are outstanding; you are a role model and have won/earned awards, credentials, or certifications that attest to your skill. People seek you out because you are so skilled.. You believe, and you have been told, that you have a gift for doing this. Anyone who knows you can see that you are good at this skill. Do not rate your interest or potential on this skill assessment. In this step, you are looking for your actual, current, top skills. You may list up to 10 skills. If you do not have 10, put down as many as you do have. I have seen people who say they feel they really only have 2 or 3 top skills. Do not put in more than 10.

Accounting
Achiever
Action orientation
Activator
Adaptability
Advising
Advocacy
Analytical
Analyzing
Approachability
Arranger
Artistic
Assembly
Attention to detail
Being active outdoors
Belief
Body coordination
Bookkeeping
Boss relationships
Brainstorming
Bringing people together
Budgeting
Building
Building effective teams
Building things
Business acumen
Campaign management
Career ambition
Caring about direct reports
Caring for others
Categorizing
Change management
Clarifying issues
Classifying data, information
Clear, engaging direction
Coaching
Coalition building
Collaborating

Comfort-higher management
Command skills
Communicating graphically
Communicating in writing
Communicating verbally
Communicating visually
Communication
Compassion
Competition
Composing
Composure
Computer graphics, animation
Computing
Conceiving
Conceptualizing
Conflict resolution
Confronting direct reports
Connectedness
Consistency
Constructing
Consulting
Convincing
Cooking
Coordinating
Counseling
Creating images
Creativity
Crediting others
Critiquing
Cultural competence
Customer focus
Customer service
Dealing with ambiguity
Dealing with paradox
Debating
Decision quality
Decorating
Delegating

Deliberative
Demonstrating foresight
Designing
Determining importance
Developer
Developing direct reports
Developing people
Diagnosing
Directing
Directing others
Discipline
Doing skilled work with hands
Drafting
Drawing.
Drive for results
Editing
Educating
Empathy
Encouraging
Entertaining people
Envisioning
Estimating
Ethics and values
Evaluating
Examining things, ideas
Expressing confidence
Expressing ideas
Facilitating groups
Fairness
Farming
Filing
Finding opportunities
Focus
Following through, up
Forecasting
Foreign language
Functional-technical skills
Fund-raising

Futuristic
Gardening
Gifting time and attention
Goal setting
Growing plants
Hand dexterity
Harmony
Hiring & Staffing
Hiring good people
Humor
Idea generation
Ideation
Identifying problems
Imagining, visioning
Implementing
Improving
Including
Individualization
Influencing others
Information management
Informing
Innovating
Innovation management
Input
Inspecting
Installing equipment
Instructing
Integrating different ideas
Integrity & trust
Intellection
Intellectual horsepower
Interpersonal savvy
Interviewing
Inventing
Investigating
Involving
Keeping your word
Leading
Learner
Learning on the fly
Listening
Making a profit
Making decisions
Making judgment calls
Managerial courage
Managing
Managing & measuring work
Managing conflict
Managing diversity
Managing negative emotions
Managing operations
Managing people
Managing projects
Managing records
Managing resources

Managing stress
Managing through systems
Managing vision & purpose
Mathematics
Maximizer
Meaning making
Mentoring
Monitoring
Motivating others
Music
Negotiating
Observing
Officiating, serving as referee
Operating equipment
Organizational agility
Organizing
Organizing people, ideas, info
Outdoor-nature skills
Overseeing
Painting, drawing, cartooning
Participating in sports
Patience
Peer relationships
Performance evaluations
Performing
Perseverance
Personal disclosure
Personal learning
Perspective
Persuasion
Planning
Planning events-parties
Playing a musical instrument
Policy-making
Political savvy
Positivity
Presentation skills
Prioritizing shared interests
Priority setting
Problem solving
Problem-solving-people
Process management
Producing
Promoting
Protecting
Public speaking
Raising-tending animals
Reading
Receiving feedback
Expressing optimism
Reconciling
Recording
Relator
Repairing
Researching

Resolving conflict
Respecting others
Restoring
Renovating
Risk taking
Scheduling
Self-assurance
Self-development
Self-knowledge
Selling
Service
Serving people
Setting goals
Setting priorities
Significance
Sizing up people
Sketching
Standing alone
Statistical interpretation
Statistical modeling
Storytelling, joke telling
Strategic
Strategic agility
Strategic planning
Studying things, people,
animals, ideas, objects
Synthesizing
Taking a stand
Talking
Teaching
Team building
Technical learning
Testing
Time management
Timely decision-making
TQM/ISO
Training
Transcribing
Treating people as individuals
Trusting
Understanding
Understanding others
Updating
Using intuition
Using numbers
Using words
Using your expertise
Visual-motor
Visualizing
WOO
Work-life balance
Working with animals
Working with environment
Writing
Written communications

Step 2. List your top 10 skills in the first column of the TOP 10 SKILLS Worksheet #8 below. In the middle column, make notes of a situation where you used that skill. Add some specifics, since many of the skills are generic. You may have skills you are not using at work, or you may use skills at work and in other areas of your life. You can share any situation where you used each of your top skills. In the data column, list ways you have demonstrated your high skill level—awards, feedback from others, grades, certifications, etc. Leave the far right column blank until the next step.

WORKSHEET #8: Top 10 Skills

SKILLS	SITUATION (specifics)	DATA-EVIDENCE	
1			
2			
3			
4			
5			
6			
7			
8			
9			
10			

Step 3. Put your level of interest for doing that skill in the far right column. Rate the skill a 10 for interest level if you LOVE using that skill. Give it a 5 if you don't mind doing that skill. Rate it lower than 5 if you would rather not use that skill, and rate it between 5 and 10 if you kind of like doing that skill but don't love doing it.

For example: Perhaps you listed among your top skills "statistical analysis," and you've taken nine statistics courses, received A's in all of them, and you are the go-to person among your friends for help with stats. Statistical analysis is clearly and verifiably one of your top skills. But truth be told, you really don't like doing stats that much. You're good at it, but you would rather do other things. You don't hate stats, so maybe you'll give it an interest rating of 4 or even 5.

This part of the assessment is VERY IMPORTANT because only you know how much you really **enjoy** using a skill. Many people will try to convince themselves that they like doing something because they do it well, other people are impressed with their ability to do it, or they don't want to be ungrateful for a skill that pays the bills. But for long-term career satisfaction, I'm asking you to be honest with yourself, even if you never tell anyone else how you feel about using those top skills. When we get to the *Career by Design* Matrix tool, you will understand why I'm asking you to be rigorous about your feelings for your skills.

Remember **WORKSHEET #7: Top 10 Motivating Interests** from the last chapter where I asked you to list your top 10 interests and associated skills? It looked a bit like this. Get out that worksheet with its lists of skills associated with your motivating interests.

TOP 10 INTERESTS	Rating	Specifics and Associated Skills
1		
2		
3		
4		

Step 4. Add your skill level for top interests on the following worksheet. I gave you more than 10 spaces because you may have several skills associated with an interest, but you may not need all of them. Sometimes you use the same skills repeatedly with your motivating interests. Remember! We are using the 1–10 rating scale, with 10 being a high interest level and high skill, and 1 being low interest level or low skill (and you can use any number between 1 and 10). It is totally possible for you to have a highly motivating interest in some area for which your associated skill level is not very high. I love to sing, but I'm usually asked not to do so in public. The love is there; the voice is not! You may have similar situations. So do your best to distinguish interest level from skill level. When we get to the *Career by Design* Matrix, you'll be glad you did.

WORKSHEET #9: High Interest and Associated Skills

Interest Level	Motivating Interest	Associated Skill	Skill Level

Step 5. Sometimes we have been told we **_need_** to improve certain skills for job-performance reasons. Go through the skills list again and select three to five skills you have been told you need to improve. Do not list skills that are already on one of the other lists. Add your interest level for the skills you need to improve.

WORKSHEET #10: Skills I Need to Improve

Skill Level	Skills I **NEED** to Improve	Interest Level

Step 6. Sometimes we have skills we **_want_** to improve for our own personal reasons. Go through the skills list one more time and add three to five skills you want to improve. Do not list skills you have on other lists. Add your interest level for the skills you want to improve.

WORKSHEET #11: Skills I Want to Improve

Skill Level	Skills I **WANT** to Improve	Interest Level

Relational Skills

If you are like many of the people I work with, you have and need relational skills but may not know how to articulate them. There is a tendency in business for relational skills to be overlooked, discounted, or lumped into a single category generically referred to as "good with people." So I developed a list of relational skills just for people in that situation. The relational skills listed here are behaviors that will help you describe more specifically what you do when you work with others to accomplish your tasks. Relational skills are skills used to obtain results through working productively with people.

Adapting—Adjusting to changing tasks, responsibilities, and environments

Advising—Suggesting or providing professional, technical recommendations

Caring—Concern for the well-being of direct reports, coworkers, clients, colleagues

Celebrating successes and achievements—Making plans to bring people together to acknowledge achievement milestones

Championing people, ideas—Taking actions that move exciting new possibilities (people, products, ideas, services) forward

Coaching—Setting mutual expectations and providing feedback and assistance to enhance individual or group performance

Collaborative conflict management—Communicating information in a manner that gains acceptance; maximizing concerns for both self and others; working cooperatively with other team members

Communicating expectations—Letting people know what is important to you in achieving the task, what they must do, and what will be the consequences or results of their behavior

Considering people's needs—Paying attention to the needs, abilities, and aspirations of others

Counseling—Understanding feelings, listening impartially, and identifying issues so that people can do what they need to do to cope and be effective

Crediting others—Giving people credit for ideas (and using their names)

Cultural competency—Demonstrating cultural awareness and sensitivity; being aware of how personal and cultural values/beliefs impact

interactions with others, and recognizing when others are interpreting behavior differently, based on differing cultural backgrounds

Customer/client care—Providing hospitality and service to internal and external customers that meets or exceeds their expectations

Developing others—Helping others to enhance their skills, knowledge, and abilities

Empowering others—Giving people appropriate decision-making authority, enhancing their skills and competencies, and trusting them

Encouraging—Helping others think and do for themselves

Energizing—Sustaining a high level of activity, energy, concentration about an idea, project, or task over time

Envisioning—Formulating and communicating a compelling vision and direction for a group or organization

Expressing confidence—Displaying and sharing beliefs that you (all) can do what needs to be done to succeed

Expressing optimism—Assisting people to see setbacks as challenges they can learn from, encouraging them to persist, try out new approaches rather than give up, blame self/others, or get demoralized

Feedback (giving)—Providing specific, timely, behavior-based information to a person about their work

Feedback (receiving)—Asking for, listening to (without defensiveness), and using information to modify/correct actions that would cause you to go off track; graciously using that information as a guide for changing behaviors and creating respectful relationships.

Gifting time and attention—Spending time teaching, coaching, listening, developing, helping others

Giving clear, engaging direction—Letting team members know what they have to do, discussing why it connects to the mission, and sharing the boundaries/limits

Goal setting—Setting SANE goals: Specific, Actionable, Noticeable results, and Enjoyable; giving people moderate challenges that allow them to accumulate successes, become more confident, enjoy the process and each other, and do their best

Including—Asking for, and using, others' ideas, talents, skills, information on projects; asking inclusive questions

Involving—Asking questions and sharing information in a way that influences the opinions and actions of others; including all stakeholders in decisions, plans, and problem solving

Keeping your word—Doing what you say you will do; delivering what you promised as a reward

Learning—Re-examining key assumptions, questioning when/whether they are appropriate or working, and fixing errors when discovered

Leveraging different perspectives —Openly asking for, listening to, and using different viewpoints; looking at issues, problems, and ideas through various view points

Listening—Giving others your undivided, caring attention (without judgment or agenda) when they are talking to you

Managing negative emotions—Using emotionally difficult situations as a chance to understand what you are feeling, why you are upset, and how you can handle it

Meaning making—Sharing insights and ideas that enhance understanding through written, verbal, visual, musical, storytelling, digital, or other media

Motivating—Letting people know when they have met or exceeded expectations; reinforcing desired behavior through positive feedback

Prioritizing shared interests—Being willing and able to go beyond self-interest for the good of the team

Respecting others—Demonstrating respect for others, and encouraging people's respect for each other

Selling—Giving information in a way that influences the external customer's buying decision or the internal customer's choice to use a product or service

Taking a stand—Sharing your views on controversial issues with conviction, grounded in both personal and organizational values, mission, and purpose

Teaching—Explaining/describing concepts or issues through presentations or discussion

Team building—Bringing together groups of people who are interdependent for a task and then providing clear, engaging direction, inclusive leadership, appropriate influence at the right time, modeling collaboration and team recognition–rewards–celebration so that team members achieve results, learn, and enjoy working together

Treating people as individuals—Paying attention to others as people, rather than as numbers, groups, or "headcount" (as if they are only heads and not whole people)

Trusting—Understanding the importance of being able to rely on each other, telling the truth, allowing people to do delegated tasks without micromanaging, keeping confidences, and being consistent in word, thought, and deed

Using names—Learning, pronouncing correctly, and using people's names (especially effective in conjunction with credit for ideas, positive feedback, and contributions)

Visioning—Exploring exciting possibilities and articulating a compelling view of the future

Win–win negotiating and integrative problem solving, jointly solving problems by blending divergent views so that all parties get what is most important to them

Invisible Work

In my research with a team of people looking at gender equity issues in organizations, we noticed a tendency for some female leaders to do a great deal of mostly invisible, behind-the-scenes work in order to short-circuit problems, while maintaining a veneer of serenity and graciousness. Ironically, since these women manage to avoid catastrophes, they rarely received recognition or reward for having solved problems . . . since those problems never occurred in the first place! The invisible work was also often invisible to *them*, their coworkers, their peers, as well as their bosses. Their challenge was to get everyone to acknowledge and appreciate the work that goes into making their effective management and leadership look effortless.

As Joyce Fletcher writes in her books and articles[5] on invisible work and relational practice, the skills that it takes to make teams work, people collaborate, and have shared learning–problem solving in organizations are often devalued or made invisible for several reasons.

First, the skill set is usually not seen as a SKILL set, but rather as individual traits or characteristics. If we think a person is born with the ability to work well with others, we (and they) often take that ability for granted. As a result, that person's efforts in developing his or her competence may not be evident, nor will other people think that they too can develop those competencies.

Second, relationship skills are often undervalued in many cases because it is hard to quantify their contribution to results. In many organizations we don't value what we cannot count. So relationship skills literally don't count.

Third, despite our rhetoric that we value collaboration, teamwork, and systemic thinking, we actually reward individual achievement, heroic efforts, autonomy, and specialization. And it is folly to hope for *A* (collaboration, teamwork, and systemic thinking), while rewarding *B* (individual achievement, autonomy, and specialization).

Fourth, we often misunderstand people involved in relational practice—thinking they are just being "nice" rather than competent and committed to outcomes. Or we think that they are hiding behind others when they talk about "we" because they're afraid to take credit for personal achievements, and that they are weaker than the big, bold, strong leaders who stand out front.

I talk about invisible work and women because there is significant and robust research that attests to women being in this situation far too frequently. This does not mean that it never happens that men doing relational work find themselves in situations where their contribution to making shared goals happen is undervalued. Whether you are female or male doing devalued invisible work that influences people to work respectfully toward a shared goal, Fletcher's research can provide a way to understand the dynamics of that devaluation.

In my book *Dance of Leadership*, I call this the Lyrical leadership style. When relational skills are developed and used intentionally to achieve results toward a shared goal, it is an empowering leadership style. Lyrical leadership, through the intentional use of relational skills to achieve shared goals, is particularly effective in situations that require collaboration, creativity, and commitment. It is an *involving* style. We find that people who have to get work done with others, or who exercise influence without control, must use their relational skills. Moreover, research supports the idea that committed performance is better than coerced performance. And relational skills involve people, so that you get committed performance. Some researchers are starting to find that leaders don't have enough power to lead effectively if they have to resort to using position power or coercion. In the long run, when working with people (as opposed to managing time, processes, or things) influencing through the use of relational skills is more effective.

I admit to wanting to give special attention to relational skills and invisible work in order to help more people see how important their contribution is and to encourage us all to acknowledge these contributions. If you recognize yourself as someone in this situation and you would like to be acknowledged for your work, I suggest that you . . .

- Refer to your relational skills as *skills*, not as traits.
- Claim your accomplishments using these skills (by putting them on your performance appraisals, for instance).
- Measure your contributions as a result of using these skills; when you make them count, others are more likely to value these skills.

Step 7. After considering the list of relational skills and reading about invisible work, you may want to add one or more of these skills to your worksheets:
- Top 10 Skills Worksheet
- Need to Improve Skills Worksheet
- Want to Improve Skills Worksheet

Be sure to add your degree of interest in those skills if you add them to a worksheet.

Intentional use of relational skills is very important in our organizations. Yet, relational work is often invisible, unless you identify these skills and keep track of your accomplishments by using these skills. If you don't, nobody else will. Name and Claim! Name your skills and claim your contributions from using them. The more you lead and manage people, the more important these skills become.

Lominger Competencies

Earlier, I mentioned using the Lominger VOICES 360 Feedback tool if you are willing to invest the time, money, and commitment to get feedback on work-related competencies. According to research and practice, specific, accurate feedback influences people to change their behavior faster than does limited, restricted, vague feedback. And anonymous, multi-source feedback is more open, honest, and accurate, on average, than one-on-one feedback. Lominger VOICES 360 gets you that valuable type of feedback.

Lominger measures 67 competencies—a blend of skills, attitudes, aptitude, and interest. The Lominger VOICES tool does an outstanding job of providing you with high-quality *feedback* on those competencies from your perspective and from the perspective of the raters you select. But it goes further by providing you with information about the *importance* of each of those competencies from your perspective and from your raters' perspectives. The VOICES competencies are also *researched* for their correlation with organizational performance, promotion rates, and competitive edges in the talent attraction area. It is most often used to rate managerial-level competencies.

The competencies are:

Action oriented
Ambiguity (dealing with)
Approachability
Boss relationships
Career ambition
Caring about direct reports
Comfort w/higher management
Command skills
Compassion
Composure
Conflict management
Confronting direct reports
Creativity
Customer focus
Decision-making (timely)
Decision quality
Delegation
Developing others
Directing others
Diversity (managing)
Ethics and values
Fairness (to direct reports)
Functional-technical skills
Hiring & staffing
Humor
Informing
Innovation management
Integrity & trust
Intellectual horsepower
Interpersonal savvy
Learning on the fly
Listening
Managerial courage
Managing-measuring work
Motivating others
Negotiating
Organizational agility
Organizing
Paradox (dealing with)

Patience
Peer relationships
Perseverance
Personal disclosure
Personal learning
Perspective
Planning
Political savvy
Presentation skills
Priority setting
Problem-solving
Process management
Results (drive for)
Self-development
Self-knowledge
Sizing up people
Standing alone
Strategic agility
Systems (managing through)
Teams (build effective)
Technical learning
Time management
Total work systems
Understanding others
Vision & purpose (managing)
Work–life balance
Written communications

Lominger VOICES 360 uses a scale of 5–1 where 5 means that competency is seen as a Towering Strength (very few people get all 5's); 4 is Talented; 3 is OK skill level; 2 means you are weak in that competency; and 1 means you have a serious skill deficiency. The instrument also asks you and your raters about the importance of those competencies to performing your job in your organization (again using the 5–1 scale with 5 being very important and 1 as not important). This means that you get an organizational culture check, and you get to prioritize which competencies to leverage and which competencies to give lower priority to, depending on importance. Of course, what is important in a current job or organization may not be as important for a future job or organization. And what is important to them may be more, or less, important to you. But we'll discuss that when we look at the *Career by Design* Matrix.

Here are a few important notes about what Lominger knows regarding competencies and performance. There are certain baseline competencies for effective managers in organizations where high skill is expected at all levels of management. These are Action Orientation, Approachability, good Boss relationship, Comfort with higher management, Customer focus, Drive for Results, Ethics/Values, Functional/Technical skills, Integrity, Intellectual Horsepower, Learning on the Fly, Managing diversity, Organizational agility, Perseverance, Standing alone, and Technical learning. If you intend to be a manager in any organization, developing these competencies will help you. Most organizations decide whether you are ready for management if and when you are skilled, talented, or have a towering strength when it comes to those competencies. It's the managerial competency wish list.

In addition, when you plan to move into higher management levels you will need Business Acumen, Command Skills, Decision Quality, *Drive for Results*, *Functional/Technical Skills*, *Intellectual Horsepower*, *Learning on the Fly*, Motivating Others, Negotiating, Organizing, Political Savvy, Priority Setting, Problem Solving and Strategic Agility. These competencies are all highly correlated with organizational performance and promotion rates. Note that the ones in italics are also in the first list. Most people seen as qualified for senior management or leadership in organizations have ratings of 4 or 5 for these skills, so you don't get much credit within organizations for doing these well. If you aspire to be a leader or senior manager within your firm, you should make sure you develop all of those competencies to the "Talented" level. This means investing in education, job experiences, training, and coaching to make sure you have those skills. Doing them well gets you considered for higher-level positions.

If you want to **distinguish** yourself as an actual or aspiring leader, you need to be talented or have a towering strength at Building Effective Teams, Creativity, Dealing with Ambiguity, Innovation Management, Managing Vision and Purpose, Motivating Others, Planning, and Standing Alone with Integrity. These are called the **Big 8** because these competencies are highly correlated with organizational performance, but hard to do well and in short supply. Being highly skilled in any of these gives you a competitive edge in your career.

There is a lot of attention nowadays on emotional intelligence; the VOICES 360 measures your competence for several aspects of emotional intelligence, including Composure, Conflict Management, Dealing with Ambiguity, Listening, Sizing up People, and Understanding Others. If you are a multicultural leader or manager who works with lots of different kinds of people, developing these competencies to the talented or towering strength level will serve you in your career (and life).

All of the information from a Lominger VOICES 360 is organized in reports that can be tailored to your specific needs. You can decide which competencies you want to have rated, and which reports you'd like to run. While the specific raters' input remains anonymous, you can get lots of statistically organized information by level and type of rater. Available reports include a Skill-Importance Matrix, the Skill Rating Overview, Comments by Raters, Hidden Strengths, Blind Spots, a Narrative of Effective and Ineffective Behaviors, an overview of behaviors that might stall or stop your career progress, and an emotional intelligence report.

I use the Lominger VOICES 360[6] Feedback tool a lot in my multicultural leadership development programs and executive coaching. Decoding the feedback with sensitivity to social and individual identity considerations is one of my particular strengths. By working with a coach, you will also receive guidance about how to develop the competencies you choose to improve. Should you decide to go this route, I would be happy to arrange it for you and help you interpret the feedback in light of your career aspirations and your cultural background. I also have other CDs and tools to help you develop your Negotiation, Conflict, and Team Management skills.

Step 8. If you have taken the Lominger VOICES 360, you may wish to return to your Skills Worksheets and add one or more of those competencies to your . . .
- Top Skills Worksheet (list only items over 4—Talented)
- Need to Improve Skills Worksheet (list any 2's or 3's that are important for your job)
- Want to Improve Skills Worksheet (list 2's or 3's that are correlated with promotion, performance, or importance to your career aspirations)

Be sure to add your degree of interest in those skills when you add them to the relevant worksheet.

SkillScan

SkillScan is an online assessment that will organize your skills into themes, link those skills to valued workplace competencies, suggest career options, and provide some practical application ideas as well as personal development and training activities. As is the case with all of the assessments I mention in *Career by Design*, you can choose to invest in the more detailed report, or you can see if you have enough guidance using the information I am providing here. I will tell you that SkillScan is widely used by a number of University Career Services for people who are trying to discover which occupations best use the skills they have, whether they are entering the workforce for the first time, after some formal education program, or whether they are re-entering the workforce having taken some time off, or considering a significant change in their career to align more with their personality, values, interests, and skills. This can be a particularly helpful assessment for reinventing yourself by using your existing skills in a new career. It is a tool I recommend highly.

SkillScan organizes skills into six categories, skill sets, and sample career options: Analytical, Communication, Creative, Management–Leadership, Physical–Technical, and Relationship. I added a seventh skill theme, Nature–Outdoors, to the list.

These skills words often end with "-*ing*" as a way to denote their action orientation. As you read the skills below, highlight skills you use, want to use, or need to use. You may not have, or need, every skill listed in a skills theme. However, using more precise skill words on your resume, in your performance reviews, and in your conversations about what you do demonstrates that you have given thought to your career aspirations.

At the end of each paragraph I mention which Motivating Interest theme from the previous chapter correlates with that set of skills. Remember! In the Motivating Interests chapter I describe not only the theme, but some common personality characteristics, strengths, and challenges (weaknesses, blind spots) associated with that motivating interest. Review those if you need to too.

Finally at the end of this Chapter I provide some examples of occupations that combine skill sets.

Analytical: *Logical processing of information and data to produce usable results.* Skills include analysis, investigating, observing, searching, comparing, calculating, programming, inventorying, bookkeeping, analyzing costs, itemizing, copying, transcribing, updating, systematizing, examining, scheduling, expediting, coordinating, following through, prioritizing, reflecting, testing, assessing, diagnosing, reasoning, conceptualizing, adapting, hypothesizing, discovering, improving, devising, problem solving, mathematics, statistics, categorizing, classifying, evaluating, managing data and records, budgeting, computing, estimating, and forecasting. These skills are used in business, finance, information systems, government, medicine, computer systems, law, marketing, research, technology, mathematics, statistical analysis, and the sciences, for example. *These skills line up with the Research, Numbers, and Data themes described in the Motivating Interests chapter.*

Communication: *Fundamental verbal and written communication skills for interaction with individuals and groups.* Skills include listening, speaking, interacting, writing, persuading, promoting, selling, consulting, editing, translating, interpreting, storytelling, critiquing, meaning-making, interviewing and negotiating. These skills are used in advertising, coaching, fundraising, journalism, HR, marketing, sales, public relations, politics, and publishing, for example. *Many of these skills line up with the Creativity theme in the Motivating Interests chapter.*

Creative: *Process, generate, and connect ideas and information into something new.* Skills include brainstorming, demonstrating foresight, using intuition, conceptualizing, designing, synthesizing, integrating, visualizing, composing, authoring, creating images, photographing, video-graphing, decorating, displaying, exhibiting, painting, cooking, crafts, acting, dancing, directing, staging shows, singing, playing music, poetry, and performing. These skills are used in all the creative arts as well as advertising, marketing, education, publishing, entertainment, information systems, science and technology. *These skills line up directly with the Creativity theme in the Motivating Interests chapter.*

Management–Leadership: *The use of organizational, managerial, and leadership skills to accomplish organizational goals.* Skills include coordinating, implementing, managing projects, organizing, planning, team building, coaching, goal-setting, envisioning, leading, and making decisions. These skills are used in business and general management, education, event planning, management consulting, non-profit management, HR, information systems, legal administration, publishing and tourism, for example. *These skills line up with the People-Leadership theme in the Motivating Interests chapter.*

Physical–Technical: *Interaction of the body with physical objects, including machines and technological systems.* Skills include body coordination, hand dexterity, observation, building, constructing, restoring, renovating, sketching, drawing, inspecting, testing, installing, operating equipment, repairing and athleticism—aquatics, acrobatics, juggling, rodeo, stunt performance, and cheerleading. These skills are used when working with computers, and in construction, earth sciences, engineering, health & medical technology, manufacturing & production, occupational health & safety, skilled trades, sports, and security services, for example. *These skills line up with the Things, and Sports-Activity themes in the Motivating Interests chapter.*

Relationship: *Interpersonal skills that directly aid individuals or groups in dealing with each other.* Skills include all the skills mentioned in the Relational Skills list in this chapter. The skills listed for relationship in SkillScan are collaborating, cultural sensitivity, conflict resolution, advocacy, providing care and support, serving as a liaison, customer/client care, counseling, group facilitation, and training. Other relationship skills are nursing, ministering, elder care, child care, informing, mentoring, tutoring, and explaining. These skills are used by mediators, community organizers, diversity trainers, travel and tourism agents, sales, business development, public relations, career and executive coaching, counseling, teaching and social work, for example. *These skills line up with People–Collaboration–Service theme in the Motivating Interests chapter.*

Another skill theme that is not included in SkillScan, but might be a theme that resonates with you is:

Nature–Outdoors: *Involvement with the earth, animal or plant life.* Skills include tending natural or cultivated plants, gardening, farming, caring for wild or domesticated animals, working with the land and its resources, and doing tasks and activities in nature. These skills are used in adventure tourism, fire protection, fishing, hunting, forestry, landscape services, agriculture, animal care, environmental protection and remediation, parks and outdoor recreating, natural resource management, oil exploration, yard and garden work, ranching, veterinary medicine, zoo keeping, botany, and recycling coordination, for example. *These skills line up with the Nature theme in the Motivating Interests chapter.*

Skill Set Combinations and Occupations

It is common for sets of skills to combine in certain occupations. For instance, you could combine **Analytical** and **Physical–Technical** skills to be an air-traffic controller, cartographer, computer service technician, electronics technician, aerospace engineer, chiropractor, criminologist, dentist, industrial engineer, optometrist, or facilities planner.

Combining **Creative** with **Physical–Technical** skills is helpful for architecture, audio-visual production, chef, fashion design, jeweler, medical illustrator, set design, sound engineering, special effects, or sculpting careers.

Add **Relationship** to **Physical–Technical** when you when you are considering catering, cosmetology, emergency medical technician, flight instruction, vocational education jobs. And add **Leadership** to **Physical–Technical** skills for commercial airplane pilot, contractor, military officer, mining safety engineer, police commanding officer, plant management, fire marshal, ship pilot, small business owner, technical director, or security consultant work. **Nature–Outdoors** and **Physical–Technical** skills are needed for activities such as hiking, cycling, climbing, camping, skiing, boating, surveying, and mining.

Analytical and **Creative** skills are helpful for art appraisal, cartography, editors, media specialists, television production specialists. **Analytical** and **Relationship** skills are useful for accountants, administrative assistants, business educator, claim representatives, credit counselors, event planners, financial planners, project coordinators, and reservations agents.

Please do not worry if you do not see your theme combination or your present or desired occupation above. There are an infinite number of combinations and permutations for skills. The ones listed above are merely a sample. In the end you want to design the career that's just right for your unique combination of skills and interests.

Some skills you will use for work; some skills you will use as hobbies. Not all skills are used throughout your career. We use different skills at different points in our lives. That is another reason why it is more important to know yourself (personality and values) and your motivating interests. Skills will be developed and dropped, used and not, at various parts of your life.

Strengths-based skill development thoughts

I started this chapter discussing strengths and would like to end it with some insights into how the strengths-based approach applies insights from positive psychology and empowering behavioral research. Strength-based skills development suggests:

1. You must own your development. Knowing what your strongest skills are boosts your confidence and encourages you to explore career options based on them.

2. You are successful when you focus on who you are, not who you aren't. Many people focus far too much on their limitations and not enough on their gifts.

3. All successful people need help—a network of developmental relationships, including mentors, coaches, friends, team members, and bosses—people who care about them, who care about their work, and who provide valuable support and feedback. Knowing who these people are and choosing to cultivate those relationships enhances your career effectiveness. Ask them for their feedback as well as their support. Feedback, even if critical, is a gift from them to you.

4. Identify the source of your weaknesses but don't focus on those weaknesses. Is the source a lack of talent? Education? Experience? Opportunity? If you lack the talent (and you need that skill to do your work), partner with others. If you lack experience or education, remedy that as you can, even if it is volunteering to do something because you'll acquire a skill you want. Lacking opportunity? My mentor David Thomas often said "*Luck is when opportunity meets preparation.*" From the outside it often looks like "they" are lucky and get opportunities that you don't get. But what I've noticed is when you direct your attention to something you want, opportunity knocks at your door. When it does, open the door. I'm surprised at how many people start negotiating with opportunity: "*Well, I asked for the chance to learn this, but I didn't want to do it now! Or in this way!*" The good news is that if you really want something, opportunity is likely to knock again. But your job is to be prepared to say **yes**! when opportunity knocks. Focus on your strengths and skills and develop your talents. You will definitely have opportunities to grow and make contributions using them.

Use this checklist to stimulate your thinking about how to develop strengths and skills strategically.

On the Job

- [ ] Seek special assignments or membership on a task force or committee
- [ ] Teach a workshop, lunch and learn
- [ ] Train or coach less experienced coworkers
- [ ] Join a brainstorming or problem-solving group
- [ ] Take on an internship
- [ ] Initiate a job rotation or temporary assignment
- [ ] Look for opportunities to make a presentation
- [ ] Make presentation/teaching videos and post to YouTube or Internet
- [ ] Volunteer

Education & Training

- [ ] Attend workshops or seminars
- [ ] Take online courses
- [ ] Take courses at educational institution
- [ ] Participate in professional forums or conferences
- [ ] Take self-study courses

Flexible work systems

- [ ] Job-share, work part-time, or telecommute
- [ ] Work on simplifying work processes to make more time for learning
- [ ] Trade less preferred non-work or work tasks with others

5. No matter what your skills or strengths, choose to do what you **love** to do, not what you think you **should** do.

At this point in the *Career by Design* assessment process you may know what skills you have, what skills you need, what skills you enjoy using, and what skills match your motivating interests while being consistent with your values and personality. If that's the case for you, fantastic! If that is not the case for you, you may need to take another step or two to home in on the right career for you.

You've now done the work to organize your insight into who you are and what you want when it comes to work. And that takes us to the career matrix for your career by design. Be sure to have all of your skills worksheets completed before you start the activities in the next Chapter.

CHAPTER 6 - CAREER BY DESIGN MATRIX

The *Career by Design* Matrix combines your motivating interests and skills to help you:
- Identify your Best Work Skills
- Design your job so that it fits your interests and skills
- Negotiate work priorities and better job positions
- Decide where to invest time, money, and energy to develop your skills
- Avoid doing work that sucks the life out of you

This matrix is the heart of the *Career by Design* approach. It organizes your strengths and skills so that you can have a career by design, rather than a career by default (as so many people do). The key point to remember in doing the *Career by Design* Matrix is that you should be clear about those skills you really **love** to use, versus those skills you learned to use but do not truly enjoy. And you can certainly love to do something but you may not feel as competent doing it as you would wish. We want to be sure to include skills associated with those activities as well. The things you love to do, no matter what your skill level, often provide clues to other talents that might be important work skills during your career.

The *Career by Design* Matrix has four parts. To facilitate the process of walking you through the steps of putting your matrix together in this workbook, I have separated the quadrants into four worksheets.

WORKSHEET #12: Best Work Skills is where you list high-interest, high-importance, and high-ability skills.

WORKSHEET #13: High-Potential Skills are of high interest and importance to you, but your skill level is lower than you would like. So you want to develop those.

WORKSHEET #14: Supporting Skills are of lower interest and importance to you, yet you are highly skilled in doing these.

WORKSHEET #15: Low-Level Skills are of lower interest and low importance to you and your skill level is low, but these skills are still required for significant parts of your work and must be done.

We end the chapter by putting the four worksheets together in ***CAREER BY DESIGN* TOOL #2: Your *Career by Design* Matrix.** The matrix format allows you to focus on what is in the four quadrants so that you can use the information strategically.

Work is Love
made visible
-Kahlil Gibran

BEST WORK SKILLS

Best Work Skills are things you do well and things you are intrinsically interested in doing. You want these skills to be at the core of your career and work life. Activities associated with these Best Work Skills should be the majority of the activities you do in your job and be how you spend the majority of your work time. This is the job content that provides the greatest likelihood that you will be effective—you will be productive (because you know how to do the work), and you will be satisfied (because the work is intrinsically interesting to you.)

Follow these instructions as you complete the worksheet on the next page.

Best Work Skills Step 1: Go back to WORKSHEET #8: Top 10 Skills. Look at your interest ratings for your top 10 skills that you put in the fourth, far-right column. If a skill on that top 10 list also has an interest rating of 10 or 9, list it on **WORKSHEET #9: Best Work Skills**. (If a skill has an interest rating of 8 or lower, it will go on Worksheet #14: Supporting Skills.)

Best Work Skills Step 2: Go back to WORKSHEET #9: High Interest and Associated Skills. If you have any items on that worksheet that have 9 or 10 in BOTH the Interest Level and Skill Level columns, add that to **WORKSHEET #12: Best Work Skills**. (The remaining items from that list will go on WORKSHEET #11: High Potential Skills.)

Best Work Skills Step 3: Complete the requested information in the right-hand column of **WORKSHEET #12** by adding information that demonstrates your competence and enjoyment of your Best Work Skills, notes about when you accomplished something significant and had fun while doing it, and experiences that make your eyes twinkle when you remember them. You want ready access to situations and stories where you have demonstrated your high interest and high skill level while using your Best Work Skills listed here.

WORKSHEET #12: Best Work Skills

Best Work Skill	Skill rating	Interest rating	**Step 3:** Best Skill Situations notes
1			
2			
3			
4			
5			
6			
7			
8			
9			
10			

Use your Best Work Skills to:
- Decide what job or projects to take.
- Get credit for what you enjoy and what you do well on your performance reviews.
- Measure your contributions and accomplishments.
- Seek entrepreneurial opportunities, if you are in business for yourself.
- Put on your resume if you are seeking a new employer.
- Search the Internet, using these skills and associated jobs as keywords.
- Volunteer—make a difference

Be sure to share the stories that demonstrate your accomplishments and contributions using these skills. Being able to talk about your deep, longstanding interest in these activities brings a twinkle to your eye that people will generally find positive.

HIGH-POTENTIAL SKILLS

High-Potential Skills are skills associated with highly motivating interests but that need to be developed. You may not have developed them yet because you do not have an obvious talent for doing those skills, you have some (emotional?) block, or you need education/training, time, experience, or opportunities to develop those skills. The good news is that you have the interest, and motivating interest provides energy to fuel actions that lead to skill development. Let's complete your High-Potential Skills Worksheet.

High-Potential Skills Step 1: Go back to WORKSHEET #9: High Interest and Associated Skills and look at items on that list where your skill level is 8 or below. Add the skills from the Associated Skills column to **WORKSHEET #13: High-Potential Skills.**

High-Potential Skills Step 2: Go to WORKSHEET #11: Skills I Want to Improve and add all of the skills from that list to **WORKSHEET #13: High-Potential Skills.**

High-Potential Skills Step 3: Look at your list of High-Potential Skills and make a note about what would be necessary for you to develop those skills: Talent? Education or training? Resources? Time? Opportunity? Put a checkmark in the relevant column if you've got what it takes. Leave the column blank if you need to take some action to develop that skill.

High-Potential Skills Step 4: List actions you are willing to take to eliminate the barriers to developing those skills in the right-hand column. Is it a lack of talent? (Make sure that you really don't have the talent but rather an emotional block.) Will you take a night school or online course? Get training through work? Make time? Volunteer to learn?

WORKSHEET #13: High-Potential Skills

HIGH-POTENTIAL SKILLS	Talent	Education	Time	Opportunity	ACTIONS
1					
2					
3					
4					
5					
6					
7					
8					
9					
10					

Use High-Potential Skills:
- For personal growth and development
- To prepare for future, desired positions
- For professional growth and development—building "competency capital"
- As indicators pointing to other career-relevant skills
- When you are seeking a mentor—learn from someone who is good at doing these activities. You are growing and you are creating a meaningful developmental relationship based in shared interests at the same time.
- To stretch—these are moderate- to low-risk opportunities to grow and improve
- To negotiate for, and receive, company support for your development
- As skills you give interviewers and managers who ask "What weaknesses do you have that you need to improve?"

This last point is a really helpful shift in career management. In performance reviews and interviews people are always asking for our weaknesses. Many people, especially women, see that question as an invitation to go into the confessional and disclose all the things they do poorly and probably don't like doing in the first place. They talk about their Low-Level Skills, which I'll discuss later. When people ask you "What do you want to improve?" don't mention your Low-Level Skills. Mention these High-Potential Skills. You're more than halfway there to making these skills work for you once they are developed because you are already intrinsically interested in them. Remember, *motivating interest* is the big factor in successfully developing and using a skill. By definition, a skill can be learned. And if it's in a performance review situation, you can actually get your company to invest in your development by negotiating for company resources toward improving these skills. Both you and your organization win.

Sometimes your Supporting Skills don't seem like work-related skills that might be useful for your organization. But with some creative, out-of-the-box thinking, they might point to a career-relevant High-Potential Skill. I mentioned earlier that singing is a motivating interest for me, yet I received feedback that my singing skills were not great. I can either develop my singing voice or pursue other ways to use my voice. When I think about *why* I like to sing, and the different skills I use in singing, such as my lyrical memory and ability to mimic sounds I hear, I then find insight into another skill—speaking foreign languages. Language skills can be career-relevant, and over the years I've developed my "ear" (a talent for languages, related to a talent for singing) into a skill (verbal fluency in a second language). It is not uncommon for your motivating interest–based skills to point to a talent that, when developed, could be a work-relevant skill. I actually speak several languages and use skills similar to those I am motivated to use with singing. I don't imagine I'll ever earn my living as a singer, but being able to remember things and speaking different languages are certainly career-related skills I value. My interest in singing pointed to a high-potential career-relevant skill.

Even with creative out-of-the-box thinking, you may still have a high-potential skill that is not directly relevant to your job or career. Many organizations have volunteer, community, or social activities where you might use your High-Potential Skills to work with others who share your interests. Doing volunteer activities based on shared interests is a great way to make and build relationships with peers or mentors. And if that doesn't work, then think of ways to develop and use that high-potential skill on your own. If the interest is that powerful, you are "called" to use it.

When it comes to developing **high-potential skills**, you must make time for them by making your professional development a priority. You make time and energy to develop **High-Potential Skills** by making sure most of your work content uses your Best Work Skills, AND by avoiding too much work using skills from your Supporting or Low-Level Skill lists I'm going to discuss soon.

Since you are not yet as skilled as you would like when using your High-Potential Skills, despite your high interest in these skills, you may lack some confidence and therefore stick with doing what others want you to do (often using Supporting Skills) so that you avoid feeling incompetent. But if you never make time to develop these skills, and default to using Supporting Skills to garner others' admiration or approval, you are making someone else happy in the short run, while discounting your own career satisfaction in the longer term. *Career by Design* is a long-term, lifelong approach to your career.

Sometimes you never will become as skilled with your High-Potential Skills as you would like to be. Because using those skills means tapping into a highly motivating interest (my definition of High-Potential Skills), you will gain energy and joy from just *trying*. In my experience, making the time to develop high-potential skills usually brings both joy and skill improvement. Often you can develop your high-potential skills into Best Work Skills. I believe that if you are deeply interested in something, you either have a talent for that activity, or that activity points to some work-related skill you could use. At the very least, you will be happier in life by honoring that energy-giving interest.

Concentrating your efforts on your Best Work Skills and your High-Potential Skills is the best way to be effective in your career. Effectiveness requires that you be productive and happy (which you will be, using your Best Work Skills) and that you learn and grow in ways that are meaningful for you (which you will do, by developing your High-Potential Skills). You will also feel empowered because you are making good choices—choosing to have a career by design—a design that takes your interests and skills into consideration.

SUPPORTING SKILLS

Supporting Skills are things you do well, but the activities are not intrinsically motivating to you. Using Supporting Skills too much in your work will deplete your motivation and drain your energy over time. Overuse of theses skills is the slippery slope to career discontent.

Supporting Skills Step 1: Go back to WORKSHEET #8: Top 10 Skills and look for skills on that list where your interest rating is 8 or lower. List all of those skills below.

WORKSHEET #14: Supporting Skills. On this worksheet, you have room for 10 of these.

SUPPORTING SKILLS	SUPPORTING SKILLS
1	6
2	7
3	8
4	9
5	10

Most people have developed Supporting Skills to survive, to get a job that pays for their basic needs, or because they have received some external rewards consistently throughout their lifetimes (such as money, status, or approval). Being in jobs and careers that primarily use Supporting Skills is the path to discontent. Just because you can, doesn't mean you should! The risk is that you will become so tired and *de*motivated over time by doing work that uses skills that are not interesting to you, there will be no time or energy left to develop your gifts, talents, and other interests.

I actually learned the lesson about Supporting Skills the hard way—and it's the reason I developed and teach *Career by Design*. For 10 years I was an international finance professional because I was good with numbers. I actually taught finance, cash flow forecasting, and accounting. But when I really checked in with what interested and motivated me, working with numbers and money was not on my list. I did enjoy the international cultural exchanges, living and working in different countries, the respect and approval I gained by having such a high-status job, and teaching. But I didn't love finance. And for 10 years I stayed in that profession, becoming more and more unhappy—and getting promoted every time I thought seriously of quitting. I did not separate what I loved most from what other people were willing to pay me to do because I *could* do it. I started in a career where 80% of what I did used my Best Work Skills, but the higher I moved up into management, the more my job content required me to use Supporting Skills, the less I used Best Work Skills, and the less energy I had to think about developing High-Potential Skills. This is not an uncommon pattern in careers. Maybe your situation is somewhat like mine was, and that's why you're using this workbook to refocus your career.

Spending your life energy on skills where you are rewarded externally (with money, status, and approval) but not internally is a path to discontent. This is the moment of a big *AHA* for many of the people I coach and teach in the leadership institutes. We often sell our life energy for these external rewards and then have no energy left to develop and contribute our talents and gifts to those activities that DO energize us—our motivating interests–based skills.

Supporting Skills Step 2: Go back and look at **WORKSHEET #12: Best Work Skills**. These were supposed to be things that you do well and that you really love doing. Look at that list and if there's anything on it that you now realize does not energize you—you don't lose track of time when you're doing it; maybe you do it well, you get external kudos and impress others by doing it, but you don't love it—move that skill into **WORKSHEET #14: Supporting Skills.**

Supporting Skills are the slippery slope to career dissatisfaction. When I talk to people who are successful on the surface and profoundly unhappy underneath, it's usually because they have, little by little, ended up in jobs they do well but don't love.

Don't sell your life energy for external rewards.

*If you don't know where you're going,
any road will take you there.*

-Lewis Carroll, <u>Alice in Wonderland</u>

Jobs that use Supporting Skills leave you too distracted and too tired to develop your High-Potential Skills. What to do, then, when your job is heavily weighted toward your use of Supporting Skills?

Since you have something you do really well but have little interest in, you could mentor another person who wants to learn these skills and then delegate these activities away.

Develop and delegate!

My coaching clients have found this to be the most helpful, practical, and elegant solution for reducing the time and energy they exert in using their own Supporting Skills. This is an *elegant* solution because you build a high-quality strategic relationship at work and simultaneously get time and energy back for those things you most want to do. An ability to develop others is a core leadership skill and almost always valued in organizations.

Caution! Avoid being channeled back into jobs that use mostly Supporting Skills. Most people will try to keep you doing what they know you can do well, without much concern for what you really yearn to do.

If you're starting this process early in your career, you have the chance to avoid being recognized as skilled at doing something you don't want to do for the rest of your career. The reward for doing a good job at a task is more of that kind of task. Be careful that you do a good job getting bottom-line organizational results, and on tasks you enjoy doing. You'll get more of those. If you are good at trivial tasks you will get more of those. If you are good at relational tasks like taking care of others, you'll get more of those. If you are skilled at doing something you don't enjoy, you'll get more of that. But even if you get externally rewarded for doing those things (and that's a big *if*), it won't be enough when you realize that you are unhappy in your life.

LOW-LEVEL SKILLS

Low-Level Skills are skills you lack and do not enjoy using. I haven't asked you to pay a lot of attention to the skills associated with things that don't interest you. Low-level skills are energy drainers. And the obvious thought might be "just ignore them." Unfortunately, we cannot always do that. Some things might have jumped out as you as things you greatly dislike doing when you went through the interests inventory and skills assessment. However undesirable, those skills may be needed in certain work situations. Some of these might be on that list of skills you need to develop based on that last performance review.

Low-Level Skills Step 1: Go back to WORKSHEET #10: Skills I Need to Improve. List those skills below.

WORKSHEET #15: Low-Level Skills

Low-Level Skills	Possible partners, ways to develop, or reframes
1	
2	
3	
4	

For me, these would include administrative detail work and copy-editing. When I was a full-time professor, we had to write peer-reviewed articles and publish in certain academic journals. I liked to design and do the research for these articles and I was good at that—those activities used some of my Best Work Skills. But I really disliked all of the copy-editing and detail work that was required to publish the final article. And I did not do that well. I would always miss some detail, or skip over some spelling or grammatical error. Detail work and copy-editing are on my Low-Level Skills list. I'm aware of them, though, because I needed the articles to be copy-edited in order to get them published. So my work content brought this Low-Level Skill to my attention.

So what do you do with Low-Level Skills? The easy answer is "Don't take a job, assignment, or task that requires you to use these skills." Even though this is an energy-draining area for you, and you'd rather not do this work, sometimes you, or someone, has got to do it.

Another option is to find partners who complement you where your Low-Level Skill is their Best Work Skill, and vice versa. You can also get this kind of complementarity in teamwork. Team up with folks where your Low-Level Skills are their Best Work Skills and vice versa. Give your teammates credit for doing what they do well—and enjoy the collaboration. Organizations need collaboration, working with and through people. So you don't have to have every skill out there as *your* Best Work Skill.

And you can outsource some of this work. My copy-editor is now one of my best friends.

And although it's easy to say, "Don't choose energy-draining jobs," in practice happy, motivated, skilled individual contributors often find themselves in this situation when they are promoted to management. They started their career using their Best Work Skills, did a great job, and got promoted into management. Now they have to let go of the competencies they loved that got them promoted, let their direct reports start doing that work, and learn a new set of skills they may not enjoy. Managers rarely like going to endless meetings, listening to excuses, being held accountable for others slacking off, giving negative feedback, and so forth. The move from individual contributor to manager is frequently a significant shift in job content from using Best Work Skills to using Supporting Skills (if you are lucky, talented, or trained) and Low-Level Skills if you are not. This process is what leads to the Peter Principle.[7]

So what are your options during the transition? Find what aspects of the skills you do *enjoy* in the job, thereby moving the skill from Low-Level to High-Potential, and then get organizational support to develop the skill through training, education, and mentoring. These have become High-Potential Skills. With time, attention, and development, High-Potential Skills become Best Work Skills. For those parts of the job you don't enjoy and you will never enjoy, you can still improve your skills enough with training to become better at doing them. They may remain Supporting Skills.

Low-Level Skills Step 2. Go back to **WORKSHEET #15: Low-Level Skills** and note possible partners, ways to develop the skill, or ways to reframe these skills with more attention on what you do enjoy. Add those ideas to the right-hand column.

THE *CAREER BY DESIGN* MATRIX

HIGH SKILL	**BEST WORK SKILLS**	**SUPPORTING SKILLS**	HIGH SKILL
	Combine your top skills and highly motivating interests	*Top skills, but not intrinsically interesting/energizing for you*	
	Core of your work Most satisfying job	Take time and energy away from developing your interests	
	• Put on your job description • Design the perfect job • Add to resume • Accumulate contributions • Articulate accomplishments	• Use sparingly • Mentor others • Delegate away	
	HIGH-POTENTIAL SKILLS	**LOW-LEVEL SKILLS**	
	Highly motivating interests, but skills need development	*Not interested/energized, nor very skilled, but the work needs doing*	
	Can become Best Work Skills Point to talent or strength	Take energy out of your work, make you feel like a failure (incompetent), reduce confidence, increase stress	
LOW SKILL	• Give these as "need to improve" in performance reviews • Negotiate for company resources to develop • Invest your time, resources, energy • Participate in volunteer activities • Link to others with shared interests	• Avoid jobs with these, if you can • Partner with others who have these as Best Work Skills • Get training and make Supporting Skills • Reframe to pay attention to what energizes you to make High-Potential Skills	LOW SKILL

The *Career by Design* Matrix helps you be more strategic in using your interests and skills for managing your career. Use the matrix to design your current job to fit *you*. Use your Best Work Skills—your motivating interests and highly rated skills—as the core of your job. Put accomplishments and contributions using those skills on your performance review. You now know what to negotiate for, what to keep in your job description. You will be ready for promotion or a plum assignment when the opportunity knocks. People will have seen you performing at your best, contributing while doing work you love, using skills you've developed. Develop your High-Potential Skills—with company resources, when you can. Develop others and delegate your Supporting Skills, thereby demonstrating that you can lead and manage effectively. And partner or team with others for tasks that would use your Low-Level Skills.

***CAREER BY DESIGN* TOOL #2: Your *Career by Design* Matrix**

The matrix will be more useful for you if you do not have a huge laundry list of skills in each quadrant. Look at WORKSHEETS 12–15 and select 3–5 items to put in each quadrant in below.

YOUR *CAREER BY DESIGN* MATRIX

	HIGH INTEREST	LOW INTEREST	
HIGH SKILL	**BEST WORK SKILLS** *Combine your top skills and highly motivating interests* Core of your work Most satisfying job 1	**SUPPORTING SKILLS** *Top skills, but not intrinsically interesting/energizing for you* Take time and energy away from developing your interests 3	HIGH SKILL
LOW SKILL	**HIGH-POTENTIAL SKILLS** *Highly motivating interests, but skills need development* Can become Best Work Skills Point to talent or strength 2	**LOW-LEVEL SKILLS** *Not interested or energized, nor very skilled, but the work needs doing* Take energy out of your work, make you feel like a failure (incompetent), reduce confidence, increase stress 4	LOW SKILL
	HIGH INTEREST	LOW INTEREST	

CHAPTER 7- TIPS AND TOOLS

The *Career by Design* process gives you information you can use strategically to *reinvent, refocus,* and *rebalance* your work life. This chapter shares tips and tools to do just that.

TIPS	TOOLS
1. Use your values-based mission statement for making decisions consistent with your most cherished values.	Mission-Based Decision Matrix
2. Plant a **S.E.E.D.** when you are not happy with your current job but you do not want to quit (bad economy, competition)—by making a **S**ideways move, **E**nriching your current job, **E**xploring other options to reframe your decision to stay, or making a strategic **D**ownshift.	Career by Design Matrix
3. Prepare a 2-minute speech delineating the direction your career has taken/is taking to use when having quick conversations with people who can help you, potential mentors, interviewers, or senior managers in your organization.	Career Statements: Career Development Statement Career Contribution Statement
4. Negotiate in your performance reviews to focus more on what you do well and on skills you want to develop.	Career by Design Matrix
5. Remember that career is only one part of your life, and balance work with the other important aspects of life.	Work–Life Balance Ratings Form
6. Make time for your priorities—people, work, tasks, and interests you value.	Time Mastery Scheduling Matrix

Let's look at these tips and tools in more detail.

CbD TIP #1: Use Your Values-Based Mission Statement for Decision Making

One excellent way to use your values-based mission statement is as a criteria matrix for making important job decisions. For example, working with my mission statement from the values chapter, "*Being with people I love, in a place I love, doing creative and expressive work I love, all with financial freedom,*" four of my values are clear:

1. people (relationships)
2. place
3. creativity
4. financial freedom

When I am deciding between jobs, assignments, new contracts with clients, etc., I use those values in a decision matrix. For example, when I was considering two job offers recently, my decision matrix, based on my mission values, looked like this . . .

VALUES	JOB 1	JOB 2	STAY
People			
Place			
Creative Work			
Financial Freedom			

I ranked each of the options by each of the values. So for people, **Job 1** had a lot of people I knew them from previous interactions and enjoyed working with. For **Job 2** I did not really know anyone. Both **Jobs 1** and **2** would require me to move away from my relational support system, so staying was actually my top choice for the people criterion: In the people row, **Stay** got 3 points, **Job 1** got 2 points, and **Job 2** got 1 point. I gave the highest number of points to the option with the greatest value to me, based on my people value.

I used a similar method for place. **Jobs 1** and **2** required moving, but **Job 2** was an international assignment that was exciting but in a big, noisy city. **Job 1** was in the United States, but in a colder climate. I love where I live and work now. So **Stay** got 3 points in the **Place** row, **Job 2** got 2 points, and **Job 1** only 1 point.

For creative/expressive work, **Job 1** involved research and consulting, using skills I have, but not very creative. **Job 2** was teaching—something I love doing, but not always as creative as what I do now. And again, I love the mix of creative/expressive work I have currently. So **Stay** got 3 points, and I gave only 1 point to both **Jobs 1** and **2**. (You can decide how to weight all of your criteria. It is *your* matrix).

Finally, financial freedom. Both **Jobs 1** and **2** were offering me a lot more money and financial security than I have in my current situation. But my core value is not financial security; it is financial *freedom*. For me that means the freedom to do what I love without taking a job that distances me from key relationships, my intrinsic creative interests, or in a place I do not love. So I ended up giving all three choices 1 point because they balanced each other out—more money and security versus less money with freedom.

VALUES	JOB 1	JOB 2	STAY
People	2	1	3
Place	1	2	3
Creative Work	1	1	3
Financial Freedom	1	1	1
TOTAL	5	5	10

Using this matrix, I soon realized that staying in my current situation was most consistent with my core values. I am also more content with staying in my current job because I know I am consciously choosing to stay. *Choosing* is empowering psychologically.

In my own life I have often changed jobs or locations because someone offered me more money, status, or approval. I would seriously consider taking jobs or assignments just because I was happy they wanted me and I had invested energy in convincing them during the interview process that I was the right person for that job. But whenever I used my personal mission statement with my values as the decision criteria, I made what I know was truly the best decision for me. I espoused values about relationships, but moved frequently based on promotion opportunities even when those moves damaged relationships. I suffered doing work I could do, but not work I loved, because somebody paid me to do it. But as I discovered, and as we move into the other parts of *Career by Design* process it will become increasingly clear to you, compromising on core values in career decisions is neither the path to satisfaction nor success.

Here is a blank **Values-Based Decision Matrix** for you to use with your top five values and personal mission statement. Consider using this the next time you need to make a values-based choice. Remember! Staying (no change) is always one of the choices to consider.

CbD TOOL #3: Mission-Based Decision Matrix

VALUES	JOB 1	JOB 2	STAY
TOTAL			

CbD TIP #2: Plant a S. E. E. D.—Sideways, Enriching, Exploring, Downshifting Moves

Sometimes you are not happy with your current job, but you do not want to quit. And promotion may not always be an option due to economic circumstances and competition in your industry or organization. Beverly Kaye[8] suggests that when it comes to a lifelong career, "up or out" are not the only options. Indeed, when it comes to the careers of women, people of color, multicultural employees, and people interested in work–life balance, research suggests that quitting might be one of the worst choices. It takes time to accumulate social capital in organizations that provides the basis for future promotions, and quitting a job where you have a good reputation may be costly.

So what are the other options when your career seems to have flattened out but you don't want to quit? Beverly suggests (and I agree) that you might plant a S. E. E. D.—consider a

> **S**ideways move,
> **E**nriching your current job,
> **E**xploring your options fully before moving, or
> **D**ownshifting.

Here are some of the benefits to each of these strategies.

Sideways move: A sideways or lateral move is a good action option when you want to do something about your work, but you do not want to leave that job. Staying with your organization can demonstrate commitment to the company in the long run, help you widen and deepen your network of colleagues, and if you pick a place in the company that is growing or moving into new markets, the sideways move can be a very good strategic choice for the long run.

Enrichment: Job enrichment is a way to reframe how you think about your work. Now that you have identified your motivating interests and skills, it will be easier for you to look for opportunities within your existing job that will use your Best Work Skills from the *Career by Design* **Matrix**. Remember to mentor and then delegate away Supporting Skills–based activities, or negotiate with your organization to have them pay for developing new skills from your High-Potential Skills area. Or, cruise in your current job and use your own resources to develop interests you may have put on hold when you were busy climbing the corporate ladder. By enriching your existing job, you can also demonstrate mastery of work (especially if your work is in a key or growth area of your company) and gain exposure to key people who will see you at your best. When growth opportunities knock, you will be ready to open the door and step into them.

Exploration: Investigating your options by looking at what's out there in the job market for your field is a good way to get a reality check. You may find that the grass is not greener on the other side. Perhaps others in situations similar to yours share the same kinds of challenges you're having at work. You may discover that there are things you can negotiate and change to enrich your existing job to increase your satisfaction. Sometimes exploration leads to a job offer at another organization, and then you are in the position of choosing to

125

stay—or go—with your organization. The sense of psychological empowerment that comes from choosing your situation can make you feel less trapped. An alternative to staying in a less than fulfilling situation makes a huge difference emotionally for most people. So exploration helps you reframe things.

Downshift: Sometimes it is helpful to take a lower-level job with less pay and fewer responsibilities—to downshift voluntarily. Many people join organizations as individual contributors, doing work they love and seeing the results of their efforts. The best workers are often promoted to management as a result. So a common reason to downshift is to leave management—with its very different skill requirements, salary versus hourly (overtime) wages, long hours, and heavy meeting expectations—and go back to contributing as an individual because the work content is more consistent with your interests and skills. Some people downshift to gain a better work–life balance to accommodate a new child in the family, getting a degree at night, medical reasons, or a time-consuming hobby. A downshift is also a good option if your current skills are dated and you want to learn new skills (but have to start at a lower level) to position yourself in a higher growth area of your company. And, finally, you may wish to downshift while you develop skills more consistent with your motivating interests.

CbD TIP #3: Prepare a Career Statement
Career Development Statement and Career Contribution Statement

The **Career Statement** is a super useful tool. It is the 1- 2-minute speech you give to:

- Get the next job or job interview.

- Have a meaningful conversation with your boss or a prospective manager.

- Introduce yourself to new clients (prospective clients, if you are an entrepreneur).

- Explain who you are and what you do at cocktail parties and networking events.

The **Career Statement** summarizes the conclusions you have reached about your career direction. In it you state your areas of experience and past value to your organization, and you put forth what you believe could be your future contribution. Such a statement is helpful because it allows you to succinctly summarize your value to your current employer or a prospective employer, or to introduce yourself to people who may be significant in your career development network.

Neither **Career Statement** is a resume, nor is it a biographical recitation of your past. The Career Statement is focused; it sets the tone and direction of actions you intend to take to support your career now and in the future. When it is done and refined, it should fit on one page.

At the end of the 2-minute Career Statement, the person you are talking to should have three positive adjectives that come to mind when he or she thinks of you, and should know whether he or she wants to hire you, use your skills, or help you.

The **Career Development Statement** focuses more on you and the direction you would like your career to take. It is appropriate for initial job interviews and at the early stages of your career before you have a strong track record for making a contribution to any particular organization. The **Career Development Statement** could also be the basic format you would use in conversations with a recruiter or in a cover letter if you were searching for a job.

The **Career Contribution Statement** focuses on your contribution to your company. It has a more executive tone, as you make it clear through your communication that you are a committed contributor to your existing organization or industry. It would also be an appropriate way to introduce yourself to executive recruiters, potential mentors, or to people considering you for significant leadership–management roles.

Both **Career Statements** describe your contribution to organizations using your skills—the focus is on your contribution, not on what you learned that helped you grow and develop. These statements demonstrate your ability and willingness to work to achieve goals. You weave in your skills. The content of the **Career Statement** should communicate to the listener:

- Who you are (employee, prospective project manager/leader, intern, etc.)

- Data and examples of situations that illustrate how you used your skills and made a contribution. (What have you done for your existing company, past companies, clubs, and volunteer activities?)

- What you want. Cite potential areas in which you could help the listener or he or she could help you. If your **Career Statement** is addressed to a mentor, coach, or supporter, sometimes the person will help by giving you feedback, asking you clarifying questions, or suggesting the next person you should meet. If you are an entrepreneur, you may be asking a prospective client to try out your services or products. If you are seeking a job, interview, new assignment, chance to show your skills, volunteer opportunity, or internship, let them know.

Although there is no single "correct" format for an effective Career Statement, experienced career researchers and counselors suggest four major areas to address:

- A statement of (continuing) interest in the organization (and why)

- A concise summary of past contributions (to that organization, clubs, or industry)

- Potential areas where you can and wish to provide value to the organization.

- A suggestion about ways the listener can support your activities and career direction.

This statement works best if it is specific and concise, factual and practical. Although it is appropriate to include information about your priorities, work philosophy, and motivation, these should be addressed in the context of the experience, skills, and abilities you wish to apply to specific activities within the organization.

Remember, too, that the **Career Statement** is intended as a basis for discussion, not as a personal sales presentation. This statement, when written, should not be longer than one double-spaced typed page. You should then practice speaking the statement, since it is what you would say during a short conversation with someone at a cocktail party, company event, or during a shared taxi ride. After sharing this statement, you want to leave that person believing that you have valuable skills he or she could use.

Career Contribution Statement—Example

(Statement of continuing interest in your company)

I've been with Sempra fifteen years in engineering and project management positions. I really enjoy the work I do here, and I look forward to the kinds of projects and opportunities I am likely to work on in the future.

(Summary of strengths and past contributions)

I started as a Field Service Engineer and progressed to Project Engineer and then to Project Manager. I have been told that I have a strong ability to assess complex situations, set priorities, and translate them into practical and cost-effective action plans. In the last two years alone my projects have come in 5% under budget and are generating 13% growth in my division's revenues. I am also recognized for attention to detail, good supervisory and team-building skills, and the ability to coordinate complex, technical, organizational, political, and personal factors.

(Potential areas for future contributions)

Given my skills and experience, two potential productive directions interest me here at Sempra. The first would be a senior strategic planning and business analysis role in determining major project opportunities, priorities, and sites. The second would be a broad management role that would involve responsibilities for, and overall control of, ongoing projects, perhaps focusing particularly on those outside the United States. Global exposure, I believe, would represent both a greater potential contribution to this organization and a closer match with my own interests and aptitudes than moving into a senior-level staff position.

(Suggest framework for future)

I know you've had some global experience, and you know a lot about our current strategic issues. I would like to have a meeting to hear more about what you learned in those positions and hear your thoughts on what direction I might take. I also know you're plugged into HR, and maybe you could help me think about how to approach them to learn more about present staffing levels and requirements and perhaps exploring the possibility of configuring a new position if that makes sense. I really love working here. I'm proud of what I've contributed so far. And I think with your guidance, I can position myself to make an even greater contribution in the future.

Now let's work on *your* Career Statement. Complete the worksheet on the next page before you start crafting your Career Contribution Statement. The instructions for the worksheet are on the page following the worksheet. And then there's space to craft your draft statement in this workbook.

CbD TOOL #4: Career Statement

	JOB 1	JOB 2	JOB 3
Position / Title			
Accomplishment(s)			
Contribution (words)			
Contribution (numbers)			
Skills Used			
1			
2			
3			
4			

Career Statement Step 1: What three important jobs have you had since you started working (or volunteer positions and roles in clubs or organizations)? List those jobs/position titles under Jobs 1, 2, and 3.

Career Statement Step 2: What accomplishments did you value most highly in each job? What were you most proud of? How does this accomplishment demonstrate a Best Work Skill? List your answers to those questions in the accomplishments row for each job respectively.

Career Statement Step 3: What contribution did you make in each job? Use words and put them in the Contribution (words) row.

Career Statement Step 4: What contributions did you make in each job that you can quantify? Use numbers and put those in the Contribution (numbers) row for each job.

Career Statement Step 5: What skills did you use to make those contributions? List them on the bottom of the worksheet. Ideally you will be demonstrating that you have made organizational contributions through the intentional use of your skills. You definitely want to include some of your Best Work Skills from the *Career by Design* Matrix.

Career Statement Step 6: Draft a statement of interest in the company. Mention the number of years with that organization, that you intend to stay, and that you are looking to move within the company (only if true). Mention the number of years in your industry/profession if you are trying to get a job with a different company. Mention what attracts you to that company if you are trying to get your first job or internship.

Career Statement Step 7: Craft a summary of your strengths, Best Work Skills, and past contributions. Be specific. Use numbers; back up your contributions from the Skills worksheets.

Career Statement Step 8: Write a statement addressing potential areas where you might make a contribution to this organization in the future. What areas, projects, and positions are you interested in? You might want to consider and mention different Best Work Skills and High-Potential Skills from your *Career by Design* Matrix in this paragraph.

Career Statement Step 9: Suggest a framework for the future. How can this person help you? When you are done with your mini-speech, what three adjectives do you want the listener to say when they think of you?

Your Career Contribution Statement—First Draft
(Statement of interest in the company. Mention number of years with that organization.)

(Summary of strengths, Best Work Skills, and past contributions. Be specific. Use numbers to back up your contributions from the worksheet).

(Potential areas for future contributions. What areas, projects, or positions are you interested in?)

(Suggest framework for future. How can this person help you?)

Read, practice, refine, and share your career statement with friends before using it in a situation where your job depends on it.

CbD TIP #4: Negotiate Performance Reviews to Focus on Best Work Skills

People are frequently surprised by how much room they have to negotiate the framework in which their performance is assessed. Many jobs do not have formal job descriptions, or they have descriptions that are outdated. Even if you have a job description and performance parameters that are current, you can often negotiate to get more credit for the effective use of your Best Work Skills that make a clear contribution to organizational performance. Notice that I am talking about contributions to the organization, whatever the size of your organization, not about your effort. Here's how it works. You need to

- Know what your Best Work Skills are.
- Use your Best Work Skills intentionally to drive results.
- Keep track on a regular (weekly, monthly) basis of the contributions you make using those skills.
- Get rid of vague performance expectations (a negotiation).
- Push back when your managers ask you to do things that are not part of your priorities/job description for the year (or add them to priorities so you get credit for them)—a negotiation.

Let's talk a bit about negotiating and the feelings it may elicit in you. I often work with multicultural managers and women who sometimes feel or believe that they cannot negotiate for things without harming their relationships with their bosses, peers, or even direct report. There's lots of research out there about how women are often reluctant negotiators. So much so, that in our Women's and Latino Leadership Institutes at UCLA's Anderson Business School, we place significant emphasis on negotiations and push-back.

She asks in formal situations. For instance, women tend to negotiate in recognized, structured negotiation situations such as buying a car. That's good—but structured situations occur far less frequently than more informal opportunities for negotiation. The exception might be moms who are very clear that they negotiate with their kids all the time. Discussing with a spouse who would take the kids to game practice, or asking a boss for a better quality hotel on a business trip, or deciding who will do what work on a team are all examples of informal negotiations many women avoid. Sometimes we are good at the informal negotiations at home, but not the informal negotiations at work.

He asks all the time. Men recognize both informal and formal exchanges as opportunities to negotiate. And the informal, even ambiguous, negotiation situations happen more often than situations involving formal negotiations. Men tend to recognize more negotiation situations, even to initiate formal and informal negotiations, about four times as often as women do. His higher negotiation frequency improves his negotiation skills, makes him more resistant to "rejections," and improves the likelihood that he will get what he wants more often than not. Constant negotiation training makes men more willing to take the risk—and it does pay off of many men. *He asks more often . . . and gets more . . . often.*

Learn to recognize various kinds of negotiation opportunities by paying attention to overwork or doing other people's work. If it is too hard to push back with your boss or peers, use what I call the "soft no" by asking for time to think about it. Use that time to prepare your response. Effective negotiators, especially those who are leaders, have broad support networks—partners, spouses, friends, mentors, bosses, coworkers, and coaches. Do the same. Consult with individuals from your support network about key negotiations. Get information from them. And practice your negotiation skills with them.

The research also says that this support network is particularly important for demographic minorities, especially when negotiating salary compensation and for performance negotiations. Network members can help you determine who's on your side, who's likely to resist you or place barriers in your way, and what form that resistance, or those barriers, will take. You can then practice dealing with others' resistance as well as any internal doubts you have.

Sometimes you have to negotiate to get the resources you need to actually meet performance goals. This may seem selfish to you, but if you don't get the resources you need to do your work well, you will not be happy or productive. You don't have to make do with limited resources or act like resources are scarce. You should assume that the organization can and will provide you with enough resources to do your job well. Make that assumption and then negotiate for what you need. By assuming you must work with the absolute minimum, you may be hampering your ability to do a good job. You deserve sufficient resources to do your best work. And so do other people who work in your organization.

Go for effectiveness, not relational approval. Effectiveness means getting results, having respectful relationships, and learning—learning about yourself, learning relational skills, learning task skills. To be effective, you have to know what you want. You cannot get what you want if you don't know what you want. Once you know what you want, stay focused on that. If you are presented with what looks like a good offer but you're inclined to say no, ask yourself "*What would make me say yes to this offer?*" Asking that question will help you identify what you want and what you need. Do not assume that people will not like you (or assume that you are greedy or selfish) if you ask for what you require to do your work, feel valued by your colleagues, and have the resources to grow professionally. If you focus on how your effectiveness is enhanced by asking for (and getting) what you want, then others will focus on your effectiveness too.

The bottom line here is to *reframe negotiations as asking*. The word *negotiation* evokes competitive win–lose thinking for many people, with a corresponding relational risk. Try thinking of *asking*. Research says that when negotiation is described as asking, differences over initiating negotiations disappear. So just *ask*!

CbD TIP #5: Balance Work and Life

Work–life balance requires us to consider how all the aspects of our lives are interconnected. What happens in our relationships affects our professional/career life and our health. What's going on with our bodies affects our interactions with our friends. Money issues can make it difficult to work out relationship challenges or to have fun and relax.

Below you will find 12 domains of daily life to which we must all pay attention, to one degree or another. Using the form on the next page, I'd like you to start by giving each of those areas of life your subjective satisfaction rating. Zero "0" means "completely dissatisfied"; ten "10" means 100% satisfied. Choose any number between 0 and 10. As you give your rating, think about why you are giving that rating and what would make you 100% satisfied with that aspect of your life. Everybody's satisfaction ratings are different. What bothers each of us and causes us to have lower ratings differs. What makes each of us happy differs. This is not an objective test. You cannot pass or fail it. Be as open and insightful as you can with yourself. What you are doing is the first step in raising your awareness about this area of work–life balance.

A few notes about what you might consider for each of the areas:
1. Health: Your energy and vitality, any health issues, diseases, warning signs, mobility issues that bother you, sleeping, etc.
2. Body: How you look, weight, hair, shape, etc.
3. Friends: Relationships with friends from all times and walks of your life, keeping in touch, college/high school, neighborhood?
4. Family: Relationships with your biological family members, extended and nuclear family, children, "friend-family," responsibilities to or for family.
5. Personal growth: Activities you do to help you grow and develop, personal growth workshops, coaching, etc.
6. Spirituality: Any religious or spiritual practice, meditation, prayer, attending religious services, etc.
7. Rest and relaxation: What you do for fun that relaxes you, expresses you creatively, dancing, writing, walks in nature, vacations, art, etc.
8. Career: Job content, status, title, respect, work relationships, responsibilities, authority, meaning in work, etc.
9. Significant other: Time for romance, sensual/intimate activity, commitment, mutual trust and respect.
10. Finances: Do you have/earn enough money? Have a sense of financial freedom? Savings? Debts? Assets? Positive net worth? Know what any of this means?
11. Home: How you feel about your private space. Is your garage clear? Is your home decorated to be restorative? Comfortable? Does it reflect your taste?
12. Environment: Country, community, sunshine, seasons, diversity, your "sort" of people, surrounding aesthetics, city/urban/suburban, views, nature, etc. Might also include your company office space.

Step 1: Record your satisfaction level with each of these areas of your life in the "Rating" column. Note your reasons for that rating in the "Why?" column. Describe what would a 10 would look like for you in the "10 would be?" column.

CbD TOOL #5: Work–Life Balance Ratings

LIFE ARENA	RATING	WHY?	10 WOULD BE?
Health			
Body			
Friends			
Family			
Personal growth			
Spirituality/religion			
Rest, relax, rejuvenate			
Career			
Significant other/romance			
Finances			
Home			
Environment			

Step 2: Look at all the areas of your life and your ratings. What insights do you glean from looking at your satisfaction ratings? (You might want to share those insights with a friend or coach).

Step 3: Look at what would be a 10 for you. That is your ideal scene. What actions are you willing to take to get you to your 10?

Here are some resources that point to possible actions you might take for each of the areas where you have less than 10.

Step 4: As you read through the information, highlight actions you are willing to take to move you toward work–life balance.

Body: The most common reason for less than 10 is not being at your ideal body weight. The weight management industry has lots of suggestions for this.
* Physical hunger
  * Eat the right foods, right time, in the right portion
* Emotional hunger
  * Watch out when you're eating your feelings. Check by using the acronym HALT: Are you really . . .
    * Hungry?
    * Angry?
    * Lonely?
    * Tired?
* Under stress adrenaline pours from the adrenal glands (hence the name), your heartbeat increases, you start to sweat, and your pupils dilate. With chronic stress you're like that all the time; eventually your body releases steroids that cause you to grow *omentum* (belly fat, to be ready for famine and a quick response).
* Life energy comes from the sun—eat foods closest to that life (not processed) and with range of colors.
* The Indian life science of Ayurveda says that we should eat the six tastes of life: sweet (milk, pears), salt, sour (citrus, yogurt, cherries), pungent (radishes, ginger, cinnamon), bitter (greens and yellows), and astringent (cause you to pucker up, like Asian mushrooms, figs, lentils, green or black tea).
* Right times: Breakfast within hour of waking (after exercise); lunch 4 hours later; dinner around 7 (sunset), followed by constitutional walk.
* Portion = size of palms; two-thirds full.

Friends: Pay to attention to who you hang out with, and cultivate your nourishing relationships. There's something called *social contagion*. We "catch" the emotions of the people around us. Social contagion is the transmission of ideas and emotions from one individual to another that increases in strength over time. We become the average of the five people we're closest to (emotionally, length of time, proximity). How nourishing are those relationships in your life?

Family: Families are simultaneously a source of strength and a source of wounds for many of us. The key is to have realistic expectations. Many a therapist's work is based on helping people deal with family issues. From a self-help perspective, if you want to explore what your beliefs and expectations of family are and bring them into reality, I suggest The Work of Byron Katie.[9]

Personal growth: Since growth activities are often important, but not urgent, it is your job to make time for those experiences. You can always listen to growth gurus using audio and video programs, or read some of the many self-help books available. I think an annual retreat is a great gift to yourself. Here are some links that offer these kinds of personal growth retreats:
* retreatfinder.org
* Omega Institute—eomega.org
* Insight meditation society—dharma.org
* Spiritrock.org
* Vipassana meditation—dhamma.org

Spirituality/Religion: Your spiritual or belief system can give your life a sense of intention/purpose/meaning. You must do what's meaningful to you.

Apart from any particular set of beliefs, most traditions agree that it is helpful to have an attitude of gratitude. Creating some practice in your life that allows you to focus on what you are grateful for and what is going well in your life can bring enormous inner satisfaction. For many young people I have worked with using the *Career by Design* process, the question "What do I believe?" can seem like an easy question. Usually they point to the teachings of their family's religion. But college is a time when beliefs can and should be put to the test. Beginning to understand religion for themselves and coming up with their own religious practice and ideology is a process through which many students go. In the Values Inventory you saw variations on religious/spiritual values you could choose. Here are some key words to consider as you think your rating for religion/spirituality that may be helpful.

Dogma is the established belief or doctrine held by a religion, or by extension by some other group or organization. It is authoritative and not to be disputed, doubted, or diverged from, by the practitioner or believers.

Praxis is the practice of faith, especially worship.

Religious means relating to or manifesting faithful devotion to an acknowledged ultimate reality or deity.

It may be that you are interested in the dogma of a particular religion, or not. You may find yourself attracted to the practices of a particular religious or spiritual path. Maybe you are not religious or devotional at all, but you do have a spiritual side. For some people the quest[10] for the meaning of life is what they rate.

Rest, relaxation, rejuvenation: Remember the 20 Things You Love To Do exercise in the Motivating Interests chapter of this workbook? Pick something from that list and do it weekly, if not more often.

Career: This entire workbook is strategies for having a career that is a 10!

Romance/significant other: The book by Gary Chapman, *The 5 Love Languages: The Secret to Love that Lasts* (and all the subsequent books in his series), starts from the premise that we all have a primary and secondary preferred love language, and that we respond (believe we are loved) when our significant others "speak" to us in one of those two preferred languages. The 5 "languages" are:
- Words of Affirmation
- Quality Time
- Receiving Gifts
- Acts of Service
- Physical Touch

Problems occur when we speak our love language to our significant others, but their love language is not the same as ours. In short, when we use the golden rule in love relationships—which looks like loving them the way *we* want to be loved—we miss the mark. We need to use the platinum rule: love them the way *they* want to be loved.

Some people may crave focused attention; others need regular praise. Gifts are highly important to one person, whereas another sees fixing a leaky faucet, ironing a shirt, or cooking a meal as filling his or her "love tank." Some partners might find that physical touch makes them feel valued: holding hands, giving back rubs, and sexual contact.

Gary Chapman describes why a person who does yard work, dishes, car maintenance (Acts of Service), etc., is floored when the significant other says ,"You never show me you love me. You never cuddle with me, or caress my hair, or make the first move for sex" (Physical Touch). Or, "Why don't you spend time with me? Why do you work so much?" (Quality Time). And, "Why don't you buy me flowers? Why don't you ever get me cards or balloons . . . just because?" (Gifts) Or "You never tell me what I mean to you. Why don't you ever share with me what I mean to you, or what my good qualities are?" (Words of Affirmation).

His books help you figure out what *your* languages are and what *their* languages are. Sometimes you have a clue to your preferred languages by noticing what you complain about most in your relationships. The books also contain questionnaires. The concern some people have with Chapman's books is that they have a strong Christian and heterosexual bias. That can be comfortable and affirming for people with those beliefs, values, and lifestyle—but quite off-putting for people who do not. I think this is a helpful framework, but because I work to be as respectfully inclusive as possible, I share that caveat along with my recommendation.

Finances: The most common issue for people who have low satisfaction scores in this arena is the desire to move from debt to financial freedom. Of course, you need to get support from licensed professionals in this area. I can recommend the following:

- Book: *Your Money or Your Life: 9 Steps to Transforming Your Relationship with Money and Achieving Financial Independence*—revised and updated for the 21st century by Vicki Robin. Many people are surprised to discover the hidden costs of certain work situations. And of course her approach is consistent with using motivating interests, strengths, and skills effectively. It is in the line of another good book *Do What You Love and the Money Will Follow*.[11]

- Website, TV shows, books, workshops, and programs by Suze Orman. Millions of people find her approach helpful.

- Weekend workshop: Millionaire Mind Intensive by T. Harv Ecker includes a lot of activities that help you examine your emotions and beliefs about money. Be careful not to spend a lot of money buying all the products sold at the workshops, however.

Home: I think of the home as an outer structure reflecting your inner realities. Does your home feel like *home*? Reflect you? What does the architecture and design of your home say about you and your family? How are the entry, movement, key rooms, cleanliness and usability of the basement/attics? Is your home welcoming, passable, cluttered, etc.?

To get some suggestions for your 10 home, consider:

- Feng Shui—an ancient Chinese system of aesthetics designed to harmonize energy in physical structures.

- Cable TV design shows

- Organizational consultant assistance to eliminate clutter.

Environment: I talked about space in the mission statement chapter. Other environmental factors include sustainability and community. One thing I will say is that most emergency help comes from your neighbors, not emergency techs. Choose a community where you feel comfortable and engage in community activity. Get to know your neighbors, and be a good neighbor.

TIP 6: Make Time for Your Priorities

In his very famous book *The Seven Habits of Highly Effective People*, Covey shares a matrix for the third habit, putting <u>First Things First</u>.

Priority Matrix—First Things First

URGENT TO YOU	NOT URGENT
1. HIGH-PRIORITY QUADRANT	**2. QUADRANT OF QUALITY**
URGENT & IMPORTANT TO YOU Performance review–based crises, pressing problems, deadline-driven projects, key meetings, prep for important presentations **1**	NOT URGENT, BUT IMPORTANT TO YOU Life balance, prep, problem prevention activities, values-based work, planning, growth, relationships, recreation **2**
3. QUADRANT OF DECEPTION	**4. QUADRANT OF WASTE**
URGENT BUT NOT IMPORTANT TO YOU Interruptions, some calls, email, reports, meetings, many popular busyness activities that are important to other people **3**	NOT URGENT, NOT IMPORTANT TO YOU Trivia, busywork, some phone calls, time wasters, escape activities **4**

IMPORTANT (right margin, top)

NOT IMPORTANT (left margin, bottom) — NOT IMPORTANT (right margin, bottom)

URGENT TO OTHERS — NOT URGENT

Step 1: Assess where you are and where what you are doing fits. Think about the activities in your days and see where those activities fit in the First Things First Matrix. How much time is spent in the all-important quadrants 1 and 2 versus the unimportant (to you) quadrants 3 and 4.

Step 2: Reframe time management now as **Time Mastery**. Time Mastery is about priorities, not about time. We all have the same amount of time. Time Mastery is using the time we have to do activities consistent with our work–life–values priorities. You decide what you want your life to look like and then do the right things to get you there.

When people say they don't have enough time to do what they need to do, they could have any number of reasons for saying that. Here are some of them. Put a checkmark next to any that sound like you.

- [ ] Not sure of your priorities, goals, values
- [ ] You focus more on what you don't want, rather than on what you do want
- [ ] You have no plan, you act randomly (in the moment)
- [ ] You lack consistency or discipline
- [ ] You feel demotivated
- [ ] You feel like a victim—you *have* to do this or that
- [ ] You are easily distracted
- [ ] You are a people pleaser
- [ ] You have too many activities
- [ ] You tend to avoid conflict (you need to push back, negotiate, set boundaries, or manage conflict)

One way to become a time master is to budget time in ways similar to how you would do financial budgeting. To do financial budgeting, you would total up money you make, note all your expenses, and allocate the money you have to pay the expenses. If you run short for a bill, you must "take" money from somewhere else or go into debt. So you can use a similar process for assessing your time situation:

* Total up the hours in a day (24)
* Make a list of the activities you want to accomplish in a day
* Divide up your activities among your 24 hours
* If there isn't enough time to cover one of your activities, choose:
>   1. to "steal time" from one of your other activities
>   2. to figure out how to streamline activities so they take less time
>   3. to leverage—go for activities that affect multiple goals
>   4. to get someone else to do the activity for you
>   5. to drop the activity
>   6. to stay stressed out (go into psychological debt)

The sixth option is not one people are consciously choosing, but by not making a choice consciously, they *are* living with the psychological and physical impact of that conscious non-choice/unconscious choice.

The second thing to do is to make structure your friend. I'm going to show you a scheduling matrix you can use as a supportive structure to help you. But don't schedule so tightly that you feel like you're in a time prison. Let the structure support you while giving you freedom within your time boundaries. Balance scheduled time with free time.

For instance, I use the Time Mastery Scheduling Matrix for activities 5½ days a week. Saturday afternoons and Sundays are unscheduled days in my week. I actively refrain from scheduling any activities there so that I have free, unstructured, unscheduled time to do what I want to do. During the other days of the week I work, admittedly some long hours at times. And I have some "me" time scheduled during those days too. The benefit of the nonscheduled time is to give space without the pressure of the clock.

Avoid a couple of common pitfalls. I've noticed in my life that when I focus on what the clock says, versus what I need to do, I feel stressed. It's not really the clock that's stressing me out, but *my beliefs* about not having enough time or not controlling my time that's stressing me out. I am always choosing what to do with my time. As are you. You are always choosing; you can choose with victim language or you can choose in a way that empowers you. Blaming time for your stress is a handy way to avoid being responsible for your choices. It's also self-sabotaging. Some choices/priorities might require patience, sacrifice, negotiation, or creativity—but they can be managed.

Personally, I don't waste time on calendars, phone systems, planners, coaches, etc., when it comes to time management. They often take more time to set up and update than it would take to do activities that are important to me. I know many people swear by them and think they work. If you're one of those, please do continue to use them (but then if they're working you're probably not reading this section). What I've noticed is that the planners don't change bad habits of reacting to other people's needs as if they were more important than your own.

Step 3: Think of your roles and goals. When you decide what to put in your important quadrants 1 and 2, think about what kind of person you want to be. Where do you want to make a difference? A contribution? How do you want to be known or remembered? What kind of legacy do you want to leave? The answers to these questions reveal your true priorities. What roles do you have where you live out your priorities? Roles are who you are; activities are what you do in your roles. Roles can be chosen by you or given to you. Roles typically change across the lifespan, and we must adjust to those changes in roles. You don't have to explain why the roles are important, but it helps to think about why they are important to you. Role #1 is SELF. Self is included because you can only help others and achieve your goals if you are take care of yourself. Set goals for each role. What kind of person/spouse/parent/boss, etc., do you want to be? Answering these questions will reveal your life goals. Prioritize those roles and goals. You start to recognize role priorities by pondering "What would I spend my time doing if I had only 2 years to live? Where would I want to make the most progress? See the most gain? Invest the most time?" This is not a bucket list of activities, but *meaningful* priorities for you.

Step 4: Break your goals down into bite-size chunks of regular activities. Small wins are the habit of major achievers. Progress toward your goals is the most motivating thing there is. Think of three to five appropriate activities for each of your roles. Choose daily activities that "fit" who you want to be. "What can I do as a 'role,' on a daily or weekly (regular) basis, that will move me toward being [description of goal for role]? For example: What can I do as a parent, on a daily or weekly basis, that will move me toward being present, helpful, encouraging, supportive, and gracious? Make these activities SMARTER—Specific, Measured, Achievable, Realistic, Timed, Enjoyable, and positively Reinforced (for you and them). SELF activities should include sleep, exercise, alone time (especially if your personality is introverted), relaxation, and recreation.

Step 5: Check your activities against your priorities and list them in the **Time Mastery Scheduling Matrix** below by priority.

CbD TOOL #6: Time Mastery Scheduling Matrix

Non-Negotiable and Fixed	Negotiable and Fixed
Non-Negotiable and Flexible	Negotiable and Flexible

Non-negotiable activities are based on your priorities; they are activities you cannot or are completely unwilling to give up. These should not get squeezed out by busyness and others' priorities. Sleep should be a non-negotiable activity (so to speak).

Negotiable activities are lower-priority activities. You'd like to keep doing them, but you will modify or drop them if absolutely necessary.

Fixed means that the time to do this activity is determined by someone else and you can't change it.

Flexible means that you determine the time you do the activity.

Step 6: Get out your calendar and use the matrix to make your schedule for next week. Start with the non-negotiable, fixed activities, since you know when they have to go into your schedule.

Then add the non-negotiable flexible activities. Choose times that work for you for those activities based on your energy patterns. Choose to do things that are important during the parts of your energy cycle where you have the most energy, the best attention and focus.

Next schedule negotiable and fixed activities. This is tricky because it looks like you may have to do this activity at a time set by someone else. The negotiable part trumps the fixed part, however. You can decide not to do that activity, leverage your time by doing something else that is from your non-negotiable side too, or push back (negotiate) to do the activity at a better time for you.

Finally, if you have time left over, add the negotiable, flexible activities to your schedule.

Psychologically, the hardest part of this process is to own that you're in control of most of your time (all of it, really). And so you have to choose what to cut when all the activities you have listed will not fit into your schedule.

Don't put, or allow anyone else to put, something on your schedule just because there's room. *Decide what goes on your schedule based on your priorities.*

I hope that this *Career by Design Workbook* has been effective for you . . . that you have gained:

- *Output*—key insights into your core personality, values, needs, motivating interests, and skills, along with tips and tools that are, and will continue to be, useful for your career journey.

- *Learning*—new information that helped you remember, refocus, reframe, reinvent, rebalance, and recenter yourself so that you grow to be the best you possible.

- *Happiness*—that you enjoyed the process and feel energized by knowing that fun and joy are actually the guides to making your most significant work contribution.

Keep in touch and let me know how you are doing.

Remember! De-fault is yours if you don't design.

Peace!

REFERENCES

[1] Mary Gentile, <u>Giving Voice to Values</u>, 2010

[2] All Birkman reports require a certified administrator. Contact me if interested.
[2] All Birkman reports require a certified administrator. Contact me if interested.

[3] To get your personal StrengthFinders Inventory, you must buy the book, obtain the access code from the book that is good for only one person, use this access code to take the assessment online, and download your report. The book will explain all of the strengths in detail, but your report will list only your top five strengths. After you have your strengths report, you may find the book Strengths-Based Careers helpful.

[4] The 360 feedback tool I use, Lominger VOICES, uses the term competency rather than skill. Lominger-measured competencies are a blend of skill, attitude, aptitude, and interests.

[5] Invisible Work: The Disappearing of Relational Practice at Work, Simmons College (free pdf download)

[6] You must be certified to administer Lominger VOICES 360. If you are interested, please contact me or another certified administrator in your organization.

[7] Definition of the Peter Principle: Observation that in hierarchical organizations, people tend to rise to their level of incompetence.

[8] Kaye, Beverly L. <u>Up is Not the Only Way: A Guide to Developing Workforce Talent</u> (2nd ed.). Palo Alto, CA: Davies Black Publishing (a subsidiary of Consulting Psychologies Press, Inc.), 1997.

[9] If you decide to explore the Work of Byron Katie and her methods, I suggest starting by watching the free online videos or listening to the audio CD version of <u>Loving What Is</u>. In the video and audio you can hear her tone-of-voice and that is important for appreciating her approach.

[10] See Quest spiritual orientation in Values Inventory.

[11] <u>Do What You Love, the Money Will Follow: Discovering Your Right Livelihood</u> by Marsha Sinetar

Made in the USA
San Bernardino, CA
21 October 2014